Mission AstroAccess

Mission AstroAccess

Contributors:

John Christy Johnson, Peter Anto Johnson, Austin Mardon,
Benjamin A. Turner, Sabryn Jones, Angela Kazmierczak,
Mehvish Masood, Manahil Jawad, Francis Fernandes, Chitrini Tandon,
Parmpreet Kang, Zarish Jawad, Ying Yi Feng, Eddrick Lee,
Margaret Wa Yan Choi, Jamie Molaro

Edited by Catherine Mardon

Copyright © 2022 by Austin Mardon

All rights reserved. This book or any portion thereof may not be reproduced or used in any manner whatsoever without the express written permission of the publisher except for the use of brief quotations in a book review or scholarly journal.
First Printing: 2022

Cover Design and Typeset by Clare Dalton

Print ISBN 978-1-77369-862-5
Ebook ISBN 978-1-77369-863-2

Golden Meteorite Press
103 11919 82 St NW
Edmonton, AB T5B 2W3
www.goldenmeteoritepress.com

Contents

Chapter 1: Introduction
9

Chapter 2: Reaching for the Stars, from interview with HR Zucker
13

Chapter 3: History of Mission AstroAccess, Goals and Gallaudet
19

Chapter 4: The Incredible Space Adventures of Dr. Mona Minkara
29

Chapter 5: Accessible spacecraft making way for an accessible earth, from interview with Sawyer Rosenstein By Angela Kazmierczak
37

Chapter 6: Disability and need for inclusivity on space missions
49

Chapter 7: Flight ops and the future, Dr. Jamie Molaro
59

Chapter 8: Space Gondolas - How are They More Accessible to Disabled People than Rockets?
71

Chapter 9: Criteria for an Astronaut, Justin Baldi
81

Chapter 10: Planning and Risk, Dr. Sheri Wells-Jensen
89

Chapter 11 - Taking Off with Dana Bolles and Mission AstroAccess
97

Chapter 12: Music and the Mission, Viktoria Modesta
105

Chapter 13: A Conversation with Caitlin O'Brien
109

Chapter 14: Testing accessibility accommodations to for disabled or mixed-ability crews operating in space-like environments.
119

Conclusion
127

Chapter 1: Introduction

About Mission AstroAccess

Mission AstroAccess is an organization dedicated to promoting disability inclusion in space exploration. In October 2021, the pilot cohort of Disabled Ambassadors were launched into orbit on a Zero Gravity Corporation parabolic flight to experience weightlessness and investigate microgravity accessibility solutions. The second AstroAccess Flight will take place on November 19, 2022, in Fort Lauderdale, Florida.

The AstroAccess 2022 flight costs have been generously sponsored through a philanthropic donation from Dylan Taylor, a pioneer and visionary in the space exploration industry. Mr. Taylor supported AstroAccess as part of his *Buy One, Give One* pledge when he flew aboard the commercial Blue Origin New Shepard Mission NS-19 flight last December. The *Buy One, Give One* pledge is a call for all commercial astronauts to consider a set of gifts that will pay it forward and support organizations here on Earth. "I am thrilled to be working with AstroAccess and encourage others to join me in supporting its vital mission to make space exploration accessible for everyone," says Mr. Taylor.

In addition to his generous support of AstroAccess, Mr. Taylor supported 4 other organizations: Edesia Nutrition, The Brooke Owens Fellowship, The Patti Grace Smith Fellowship, and Space for Humanity.

More details about AstroAccess can be found on their website at https://astroaccess.org/. Information can also be found by following Mission: AstroAccess on your favorite social media site.

About Zero Gravity Corporation

Zero Gravity Corporation is a privately held space entertainment and tourism company whose mission is to make the excitement and adventure of space accessible to the public. The experience offered by Zero-G gives individuals the opportunity to experience true "weightlessness" without going to space. Zero-G's attention to detail, excellent service and quality of experience combined with its exciting history has set the foundation for exhilarating adventure-based tourism. You can learn more by visiting the Zero-G website at www.gozerog.com.

Rationale

This book serves to outline the stories and perspectives of those who participated in this historical initiative. Several of the authors have shadowed, interviewed, and studied the members of the Mission AstroAccess crew and have been involved in extensive research surrounding the mission, the team, and their backgrounds. Over the course of this book, we will be introduced to several characters that have played critical roles in the shaping of Mission AstroAccess.

Overview

Here is a brief overview of the crewmates interviewed and their roles/responsibilities within the larger Mission AstroAccess context. Additionally, we have included chapters specific to disability and space accessibility in line with Mission AstroAccess including chapters on policy and space gondolas. The following list is a list of interviews and a brief description of the interviewee. The square brackets indicate the interviewer.

[Sabryn Jones] HR Zucker: HR does most of our interactions with disabled vet organizations.

[Zarish Jawad] Mary Cooper: Mary was on flight one. She has an artificial leg and she's now doing a student internship at Space X. One of the things she is working on is a kind of boot jack: a thing you could use in zero G to make it easier to take your leg on and off. She is also flying on #2 this fall.

[Angela Kazmierczak] Sawyer Rosenstein: Sawyer is in a wheelchair and was on flight one. He is a space reporter, has met a bunch of astronauts and has dealt with accessibility as a journalist trying to cover launches.

[Mehvish Masood] Mona Minkara: Mona is now the blind person on the planet with the most Zero G experience. She also has a YouTube channel called "Planes, Trains and Canes" where she documents her travels as a blind person--it's super cool!

[Manahil Jawad] AJ Link: AJ is the Mission's communications director. He is 39; openly autistic; (his wording) and has a degree in space law... and he runs disability training. We talked to him about a way of standardizing how we talk about disability: what kinds of language we use and more.

[Francis Fernandes] Jamie Molaro: Jamie is running flight ops for the crew this time and co-chaired flight ops the first flight. She knows everything about the experiments that were done aboard that flight.

[Chitrini Tandon] Justin Baldi: Justin is the (not disabled) ASL interpreter who flew on flight one. He does all kinds of cool things. He works at NASA doing ASL. He and Apurva Varia have flown twice together, and they did some research about ASL in zero G.

[Parmpreet Kang] Viktoria Modesta: Viktoria has a one-leg amputation. She's also a professional singer/dancer. She has LOTS to say about your body and disability. You should listen to her music. She flew twice and worked on new kinds of artificial legs for zero G. She calls herself a bionic pop artist.

[Eddrick Lee] Dana Bolles: Dana was in the wheelchair group. She works for NASA in education and outreach.

[Nasia Sheikh] Zuby Onwuta: Zuby is a business owner. He created a pair of glasses with a brain interface: I think gamers have these. He wants to use these to give disabled people hands free access to things like GPS. He's blind and was on flight one.

[Benjamin Turner] Caitlin O'Brien: Caitlin was on the ground crew and did all kinds of logistics.

[Margaret Wa Yan Choi] Space gondolas - how are they more accessible to disabled people than rockets?

Chapter 2: Reaching for the Stars, from interview with HR Zucker

Sabryn Jones

The dream of reaching the stars is one that most children have. As humans, we are fascinated by space, and what lies beyond the moon we look upon every night. We wish on stars and find comfort in what lie beyond our universe. Countless media and art is based on the questions that we find ourselves asking. For most of us, those dreams will never be much more than a fantasy we think back on. We grow up - and do what is expected of us. In the case of HR Zucker, anything that had yet to be explored just meant that he had the opportunity to do it himself. As a child, he saw humans reach space and walk on the moon for the first time. In his childlike wonder and awe, HR knew that he wanted to push limits and make his mark on the world. He does all this and more, leading an incredible life full of firsts and genuine kindness. HR worked under the chain of command of the US Government, navigating a way into space travel and seeing a gap in the people who are able to fly. A life that most people only read about in magazines was born out of tenacity and the daring to ask if he could try.

When I meet HR for the first time, his Zoom background is set to a picture of a satellite in space. A US flag pin is neatly placed on his suit jacket's lapel alongside another pin I can not quite make out. His greeting is kind and warm, and he is excited to chat with me despite having very little idea of who I am. It only takes one question, "why are you passionate about getting people in space?" for him to nod and begin his answer, which lasts about twenty minutes, with me saying very little. He starts with his childhood, stating that he had been enamoured by the heavens as a baby. Seeing so much movement in space as a child ignited a passion in him, coupled with the nature to "explore and see new things, at least I hope folks like to have that." He says of the new technology of air and space. Zucker had his start in aviation. To be more specific, his career was in the air force and electronic warfare. He went through all the basics of flight school and learned all he could within our atmosphere, but Zucker felt in his heart that the future was still in space. By this time in the 1980s, there was "no clear path for a person who was in the flying world to go into the space world" outside of some very specific and narrow ways one could ever hope to accomplish that. Zucker knew he wanted his career to take him into space. With hard work and people backing him up (a four-star general permitting him to try, for example), Zucker was able to join the force of people who work with and in space.

Since then, Zucker has had the opportunity to work on a novel technology that protects us from attacks in space, for example, anti satellites. Zucker recalls, "my first space job was working on an F-15 that was going to take a space vehicle - take off from a runway and launch something into space to defend the US against any capability that was going to hurt us." There is a particular pride behind every word. The knowledge that was he did was the stepping stone for what space technology is now and what it might look like in the future. He is never boastful but rather excited to share the stories that got him here. Zucker admits that they learned very quickly that breaking down the material in space is not healthy or sustainable. Under former US President Ronald Regan, Zucker was working through the chain of command directly to the Whitehouse. The program Zucker worked on had to be cancelled, forcing everyone to try and rethink what their next steps would be and how to avoid going backwards. Zucker tells me a bit about his friends who worked within the military with him - some of who went on to be highly recognized and respected. Many of them he had worked with for years, growing up with and praising the work that his colleagues have accomplished. He finishes his slight sidetrack with a smile and says, "it's kind of funny how life is."

Zucker worked on the experimental development and planning, alongside his boss, of the space shuttle. He worked under the Space Defence Initiative Organization (SDIO), which Zucker affectionately called 'Star Wars', and he absolutely lights up as he talks about his job was to experiment with lasers from space. It is the type of job little kids dream about, and the excitement in his voice is evident. His career was chalked full of experiences like these - he never turned away from something that seemed new or unsure. He brushes over the years he spent away from space travel and a very brief mention of the Gulf War and how uncertain he felt space travel would be again. The way he started working with AstroAccess and getting people with disabilities in space is something else entirely. In the 90s, his brother had jokingly said to him, "if you want to go to space, why don't you buy your way in?" While it was just a sibling taunt, that reality started to form while Zucker was working in international protection and space defence.

His dream had always been to be an astronaut, and coming back to the first instinct made sense after all the success he had seen. Upon hearing that Stephen Hawking was offered a chance to fly while being a wheelchair user, Zucker asked himself what he could do that could be that meaningful and impactful. It brought him back to thinking of an old classmate of his. They had grown up together and were perfectly healthy and able-bodied. Unfortunately, roughly three weeks after graduation, the classmate had an injury that paralyzed him, and he never fully recovered. Zucker had reached out to him, and in his own words, said, "I'm going to throw something crazy at you…How would you like to go into space?" The classmate agreed, and something was born. From there, it was a question of how to raise the funds and who to reach out to to see if this was possible. More or less, this is Zucker's role within AstroAccess to this very day. He makes connections and gets the funding as they need it. Most of what he does is within the back end of the business, but he seems to be totally okay with this. He cares more about the bigger picture than anything else. With some connections from past conferences, Zucker was able to meet with the CEO of Virgin Galactic. With the interest of Virgin Galatic, it took about a year before the ball started rolling, and Zucker was having meetings with other individuals who were interested. It ultimately would be these connections that would allow AstroAccess to take off, with Zucker helping in any way he could.

Zucker stops himself before continuing with the origin story of the organization. "Me being the eager beaver…." he starts to delve into the process of naming the organization. The names he offered up included Disability Access in Space or DAIS. The name did not stick for this organization, but he tells me with a smile that he saw the name DAIS pop up again a few months later when another organization took the name. He laughs and calls it two parallel universes. Quickly, he goes back to the main story and explains that the number of people involved started to grow. AstroAccess had its first mission in October in Long Beach, California. Whatever needed to be done, Zucker was willing to help out and keep the back ends of the project running. He compared it to babysitting in that you have to nurture something to see the results that you want - even if others are more of the parents or faces of it than you.

It is important to note that Zucker himself is not disabled and does not identify as such. Instead, he admits that he is still learning the language and admits to being an outsider looking in. "It takes time to build trust in things you don't understand," he says of working with people who are disabled. With his extensive background in what is referred to as 'old space', he knows that the world of space has been closed off for too long. 'Make space for everybody' sums up his feelings towards the whole conversation. I can see how much he cares and believes in this when talking to Zucker. His entire life has been full of learning, and he does not seem to be slowing down at any point soon. The T-shirts and patches that Astro-Access wear are designed by artists with disabilities. Zucker happily shows me the real patch that they use, an image of a dog wearing a space suit. It is a clever nod to the nickname that he gives the teams when they go on missions. 'Crew Dogs' is a term that he uses for team building and giving a sense of culture and belonging. He also happily shows me the jacket they wear; it seems like he keeps his close to the back of his office chair, so it is always ready for the next adventure. He interacts with his team the way he would have on a combat mission - he gives the mission a sense of community and excitement for everyone involved. For those who could not hear, they have interpreters on the bus to keep it inclusive. He tells me that he hopes that he introduced that memory of what it was like to be a 'Crew Dog' to each of them.

It is clear that HR Zucker feels a sense of fulfilment in being able to share space flight with those who may not be able to otherwise. In his words, even when he flies his airplane, he hates flying alone. He finds it tedious and would rather have someone up there with him. As I wrap up the interview, he takes the time to get to know me rather than simply logging off. We chat about my disabilities, and he encourages me to apply to be an ambassador. With knowing very little about me, it seems essential to him that he thanks me for writing and sharing my gift with the world. I am blown away by his kindness and humble nature, a stranger being so encouraging to someone who does not even live in the same country as him. Yet, when it boils down to it, that is really who HR Zucker is. He is a man who simply cares, who wants to learn about everything and everyone on this Earth and get to share those experiences with as many people as he can.

His life is something that most people will never experience. Every opportunity he had has seemed only to inspire him to keep going forward. Zucker has yet to fly into space himself, but his life has been dedicated to letting others have that experience. He does still hope to do day see the stars and add that to the list of dreams that he can now check off. AstroAccess is something he believes in full and something he put the groundwork in for years ago. AstroAccess has the ability to live beyond him and everyone else involved, and that is what he hopes for it. If the proper work is put in now, it could be more than the people involved and about what the organization stands for that withstands the test of time. Zucker might not be an astronaut, but the sheer amount of people he has helped send into space and the lives he has affected have made the most significant impact amongst the stars.

Chapter 3: History of Mission AstroAccess, Goals and Gallaudet

Zarish Jawad

Over 500 people have flown to space since the beginning of human spaceflight in the 1960s; however, individuals with disabilities have largely not been considered for spaceflight in the history of space exploration (Morris, 2021). A reason for the exclusion of individuals with disabilities in space missions and exploration are the strict standards and prerequisites for physical requirements set by various space agencies including the National Aeronautics and Space Administration (NASA) and other private space agencies. NASA's initial criteria for selecting astronauts included white, physically fit men (Lewis, 2021). Despite broadening its criteria, it still chooses people who meet certain physical requirements, thus blocking the path to space for many individuals with disabilities.

However, human spaceflight is experiencing a major transformation as the rise of commercial spaceflight has challenged the conventional definition of an astronaut (Lewis, 2021). New possibilities in space missions are being created with the rise of funded private spaceflight and with the support of government space agencies, permitting a much wider and more diverse pool of people to take part in trips to space, including individuals with disabilities. Initiatives, activities and ventures are underway to make space travel accessible for people with disabilities, such as NASA's Parastronaut Feasibility Foundational Research Study issued in November 2021.

The study investigated the feasibility of sending people with disabilities safely into space and returning them to Earth (Richardson, 2022). The European Space Agency (ESA) "Parastronaut Feasibility Project," announced in February 2021, sought to hire a parastronaut which is centered on the inclusion of persons with a physical disabilities while still ensuring that the space mission is productive and safe. They undertook the inspiration4 mission by SpaceX in September 2021 with the first prosthesis (Richardson, 2022).

Another step towards inclusion of individuals with disabilities in space missions was with Hayley Arceneaux. Hayley Arceneaux in space and mission AstroAccess conducted a parabolic flight in October 2021 with twelve veterans, scientists, students, artists and athletes with disabilities. Arceneaux along with the team were launched into a zero-gravity environment and the aim of this first step was to understand the environment and what is required to make space inclusive for all, especially for individuals with disabilities. Finally, it aimed to find methods to make designs more accessible to allow crewmembers with disabilities to complete the necessary work in microgravity.

Often the requirements or the ideal candidate for an astronaut is an individual who is strong, smart and adaptable because traveling to space can be physically and mentally challenging. People who can easily adapt to various situations and worlds are the best at being adaptable and flexible. Individuals with disabilities are adaptable and flexible because they navigate difficult situations every day. Therefore, we can say that individuals with disabilities have inherent strengths and advantages that could enhance mission success. This was tested and proved long ago in the 1950s. Individuals who are deaf have differences in their vestibular system, making them less immune to motion sickness. NASA knew this when 11 deaf men participated in extensive research to help shape the future of human space exploration.

These men were known as "Gallaudet 11". During these experiments and research, NASA proved that deaf space flight participants would be more adaptable to foreign gravitational environments. But yet, there has never been a deaf astronaut on a space mission. According to Hannah Hotovy of the NASA history division, the work of the Gallaudet Eleven made significant contributions to understanding adaptation and motion sickness to spaceflight. There are other reasons which support that bringing deaf astronauts to space missions could be useful.
 In addition, as per Joseph Murray, a professor at Gallaudet University, sign language provides a cognitive advantage as it enhances an individual's working memory and the way individuals remember, observe and manipulate objects in their minds. Individuals who are deaf are always willing to be part of space missions that require individuals immune to motion sickness and those with advanced spatial processing skills.

ESA called for parastronauts or astronauts with physical disabilities (qualified individuals with certain disabilities) as the agency wants to make its new astronaut class more gender diverse than ever. Still, it will take redesigned gear to make space accessible to everybody including individuals with disabilities. ESA started accepting astronaut applications from individuals with leg amputations or candidates with deficiencies in both feet, legs, lower limbs, amputations, or individuals with differences in the length of their legs or individuals who are less than 130 centimeters (4 feet, 3 inches) tall. ESA hopes to expand and include more types of disabilities in their criteria in the future. After completing the selection process, the next few years will be spent by the ESA officials figuring out how to make their parastronaut program workable with the agency's US and Russian partners and what all internal spacecraft modifications might be required. ESA is also overseeing the development of the ESM (European Service Module), the part of the Orion spacecraft of NASA, which will provide electricity, air and propulsion during a future Orion flight to the moon and back. Therefore, meaning that astronauts with disabilities have to ride inside a spacecraft operated by NASA, Russia's space agency, or a private firm like SpaceX. The push for diversity has been welcomed by various space agencies, but the concept of a parastronaut is also well taken as it will open the doors to a population that has mostly been ignored in space exploration, individuals with physical and other types of disabilities. Seeking diversity in space is as equally important as diversity in any other setting or place.

In July 2021, the SciAccess initiative, which works to make science, technology, engineering and mathematics (STEM) through a series of programs, announced its Mission AstroAccess for individuals with disabilities who have always dreamt of training to fly to space. The initiative opened up applications to crew participants with disabilities for a Zero-G parabolic flight. Under this program, a diverse group of individuals with disabilities fly on a parabolic flight using a series of parabolas to create weightlessness in the plane's cabin aboard the Zero Gravity Corporation (Zero-G) 's "G-Force One" plane. With this flight(which eventually took place on 17 October 2021), the program hopes to expand the crew's knowledge and understanding of how individuals with disabilities can safely travel and work in space, thus making space more accessible and inclusive for all.

According to George Whitesides, mission project lead, "With this flight, we hope to lay the foundation for future disabled space explorers." Whereas Anna Voelker, mission project lead and executive director of the SciAccess Initiative and the Aspen Science Center, said,

"Implementing accessibility is crucial not only for inclusion but for the safety and success of all space explorers." Mission Astroaccess, an initiative dedicated to "advancing disability inclusion in space," made history on 17 October 2021 when a zero-gravity flight was launched with a team comprising of twelve disability ambassadors, who tested design solutions to make spaceflight accessible to people with mobility, vision, and hearing disabilities. These ambassadors were competitively selected, resulting in representing a diversity of backgrounds, careers, and abilities. There were two deaf, six blind, and four mobility-impaired members.

The team flew aboard a Zero Gravity Corporation parabolic flight, which creates sensations of microgravity and hypergravity through its flight path. Weightlessness lasted only for around 20 seconds, but the passengers experienced it 15 times as the plane flew up and down repeatedly. In a press conference the day after the mission, co-project lead George Whitesides said, "Space should be accessible for all. We are on the verge of an incredible moment in human history when ... space opens for the benefit of humanity, and we have to take everyone with us—that future has to be inclusive."

On a zero-gravity research flight, people with different types of disabilities tested their skills and technologies to prove they could safely travel to space. The ambassadors, scientists, consultants, veterans, students, athletes, artists and CEOs, used their experiences to recommend solutions to their challenges. The inaugural flight focused on basic operational tasks to reveal the abilities of disabled crew members to work effectively in microgravity and investigate solutions for better accessibility. One of the goals of this flight was to test ways to make spacecraft accessible by design for which, in the name of science and a more accessible final frontier, 12 people with various disabilities floated weightless in simulated space environments. Besides seeing how people with different types of disabilities deal with the demands of partial and zero gravity, another goal was to find barriers to accessibility in existing space flight environments.

In addition, AstroAccess investigated challenges associated with physical environment accessibility communication and safety procedures in space. According to Ann Kapusta, AstroAccess mission and communication director, with just a few modifications for each type of disability, the dozen participants in the flight had a roughly 90% success rate of getting back to their seats after 15 tests, 12 tests in zero gravity, two that mimicked lunar gravity and one that mimicked Martian gravity (Gohd, 2021).

Furthermore, researchers tested special lighting systems for deaf passengers, navigational devices, Braille for blind passengers, and modified spacesuits for impaired mobility passengers. Researchers described the unique strengths and resilience that individuals with disabilities bring to a space mission (Eveleth, 2019). An inclusive design consultant, Bahram spoke to the constant problem-solving skills individuals with disabilities require in the inaccessible space: "In a day, most disabled folks solve more problems than non-disabled folks do in a month." It was a consensus among the participants of the 17th October flight, and they argued that accessibility issues must be considered now at the advent of private space travel rather than later because higher investment of time and money is required to make retrofitting equipment more accessible.

Currently, the Federal Aviation Administration is barred from creating safety regulations for private space flights until October 2023; however, initiatives like AstroAccess aim to guide how government agencies think about accessibility on spaceflights. According to Eric Ingram, wheelchair user and one of the ambassadors of accessibility in space missions, "It's important to prevent misinformation and overcome a lack of data from making bad regulations that would prevent someone with disability from flying on one of these trips" (Tim, 2022). Therefore, it is equally important that people with disabilities, besides just claiming a space for participation in space travel, are also involved in the critical planning stage. As per Sawyer Rosenstein, a journalist, a spacecraft can be easily made accessible and modified for individuals with disabilities, including spacecraft design and avoid expensive retrofitting (David, 2021). Many private space flight companies are interested in being part of the mission and can do many things proactively to make the designs of spacecraft more accessible. Moreover, Amanda Morris, a disability reporting fellow, also believes that it is critical to make spaceflight accessible now while private space flight is opening up. More importantly, individuals with disabilities should be included at every step of the planning process.

After parabolic flights, the goal is to fly suborbital and officially reach outer space. But for that specific purpose, it must continue with more Zero-G flights to test and develop technology, besides researching to ensure the safety and security of the people with disabilities on board spaceflight (Gohd, 2021). Such ventures and initiatives provide the opportunity to view individuals with disabilities as role models and to ensure their place and inclusivity in space. Including disabled personnel will call for changes in space habitats, equipment, policies, and procedures that will benefit everyone. Initiatives, ventures and activities undertaken by NASA, ESA, through Mission: AstroAccess and other private space firms and organizations are the steps in the right direction for the bright future of individuals with disabilities and increased accessibility for space missions (Morris, 2021). Once individuals with disabilities are provided the opportunity to showcase their skills and learn their strengths and capabilities for space exploration, NASA and other private companies will begin working more vigorously towards accessibility and ensuring a space for individuals with disabilities in their astro missions.

References

Morris, A. (2021, October 22). *A future for people with disabilities in Outer Space Takes flight*. The New York Times. Retrieved September 3, 2022, from https://www.nytimes.com/2021/10/22/science/astronauts-disabilities-astroaccess.html

Lewis, B. (2021, December 30). *Mission: AstroAccess is making space accessible for all*. astrobites. Retrieved September 3, 2022, from https://astrobites.org/2021/12/24/mission-astroaccess-is-making-space-accessible-for-all/

Richardson, B. (2022, March 7). *The future of space will be ADA accessible thanks to mission: Astroaccess • long beach business journal*. Long Beach Business Journal. Retrieved September 3, 2022, from https://lbbusinessjournal.com/aerospace/the-future-of-space-will-be-ada-accessible-thanks-to-mission-astroaccess

Gohd, C. (2021, July 20). *Disabled space enthusiasts can now apply for Zero gravity space training*. Space.com. Retrieved September 3, 2022, from https://www.space.com/astroaccess-zerog-flight-disabled-astronaut-training

David, L. (2021, December 31). *Equal Access to Space: New Study investigates how to get more 'Parastronauts' aloft*. Space.com. Retrieved September 3, 2022, from https://www.space.com/inclusive-human-spaceflight-parastronaut-study

Eveleth, R. (2019, January 27). *It's time to rethink who's best suited for Space Travel*. Wired. Retrieved September 3, 2022, from https://www.

wired.com/story/its-time-to-rethink-whos-best-suited-for-space-travel/

Tim Gilmer. (2022, April 18). *The wheelchair users helping make space flight accessible*. New Mobility. Retrieved September 3, 2022, from https://newmobility.com/the-wheelchair-users-helping-make-space-flight-accessible/

Team, reillymurtaugh | T. S. T. (2022, July 15). *AstroAccess makes space travel accessible for disabled people*. TheSocialTalks. Retrieved September 3, 2022, from https://thesocialtalks.com/science/astroaccess-makes-space-travel-accessible-for-disabled-people/

Chapter 4: The Incredible Space Adventures of Dr. Mona Minkara

Mehvish Masood

One of the incredible Astro Access Ambasadors is Dr. Mona Minkara, a blind scientist who has experienced an amazing journey of trials and tribulations. Her perseverance has led her to become a professor at Northeastern University and has enabled her to engage in various activities. One of these projects involved becoming an Astro Access Ambassador. In this role, Mona has taken part in three parabolic flights to gain an understanding of how to increase accessibility for the visually impaired. This makes her the blind person with the most zero gravity experience on the planet!

Background

Mona Minkara was born in Maryland and was brought up in the Boston area. When she was seven, she was diagnosed with macular degeneration and cone-rod dystrophy, which eventually caused her blindness. While there were many to discourage Mona, her parents stood by her side and encouraged her throughout her journey. She pursued an education in the Massachusetts public school system and, towards the end of high school, started to realise something far greater: her potential could far exceed that of what society expects of a blind individual. She took advanced classes and had incredible success.

Driven by a need to continue her academic exploration, Mona continued advanced classes until she entered her post-secondary education. She was accepted to Wellesley College with scholarships and met people that allowed her to broaden her understanding of the world. She double majored in Middle Eastern Studies and Chemistry and was initially undecided about which path to take, but ultimately decided to pursue science. She received the National Science Foundation Research Experience for Undergraduates award during her first summer as an undergraduate researcher under Dr. Coleman. Subsequently, receiving the same award every summer as an undergraduate student, she worked in the lab of Dr. Mala Radhakrishan where she explored drug binding to HIV-1 reverse transcriptase. This experience had a huge impact on Mona as she realised that she wanted to pursue scientific research after this.

Mona decided to continue doing research for a year after graduating from Wellesley College. Following this, she was awarded a National Science Foundation Graduate Fellowship. Consequently, she moved to the University of Florida for her Ph.D in Chemistry, where she focused her research on biological systems and computational chemistry-aided drug designs. While it was not a requirement of her fellowship to be a teaching assistant (TA), Mona decided that she wanted to try to get some experience. Her request to be a TA was met with apprehension by the Chemistry Department due to her blindness, but she was eventually chosen to be the first blind TA at the University of Florida. This ended up being one of the best experiences of her life, with students giving incredibly positive feedback. One of her student testimonials stated: "Were Mona a professor, I would go out of my way to take another class with her. I was very impressed, to say the least, as well as humbled and inspired by her courage and fortitude."

Following her experience at the University of Florida, she joined Professor J. Ilja Siepmann at the University of Minnesota. Upon completion of her postdoctoral work, Mona moved back to Boston and became a Bioengineering professor at Northeastern University, starting in August 2019. Mona taught Biomolecular Dynamics and Control alongside pursuing research that she was passionate about. Being one of the first blind professors in the department, teaching this course was initially a challenge because Mona did not have any examples of other blind professors teaching the class. However, she found a way to overcome this challenge by making her own teaching system that worked for her and her students. Till now, Mona has continued teaching at Northeatern University. She has used her love of teaching to help students and propagate change in society by showing that having a blind professor in a visual field is possible. She has won multiple teaching awards, including the Martin Essigmann Outstanding Teaching Award at Northeastern University.

Projects and Achievements

Mona has continued her journey to accomplish incredible achievements throughout her life. She has been involved in many different projects and has been the recipient of various highly impressive awards. Many of her initiatives have involved bringing awareness to and advocating for the visually impaired. This section will outline some of these accomplishments.

Mona is the creator and director of *Planes, Trains, & Canes (PTC)*, an award-winning Youtube channel to explore public transportation and visit interesting places around the globe. Some of the locations she has visited include Japan, Singapore, London, Istanbul, and Johannesburg. The team that helped Mona in creating her extraordinary videos includes Natalie Guse, Benjamin Ted, Dr. Elizabeth Janney, and Afridi

Shaik. Her impressive insights on this channel has won her the Holman Prize. This competitive award is won by three blind individuals every year by ambitious individuals that "challenge themselves and shatter misconceptions about blindness around the world."
Follow @planestrainsandcanes on social media to get more information.

Moreover, Mona partnered with a STEM team in 2016 to conceptualise and design a STEM curriculum for blind individuals. This curriculum is accessible to both visually impaired and sighted learners, and provides a collection of hand-on lessons for young learners. With a constructive educational approach, the Blind STEM curriculum encourages students to explore and experiment with our physical world through the use of collaboration. There is an emphasis on using all senses and a focus on utilising low-cost, accessible materials in underserved regions. This curriculum gives a different perspective and challenges the visual approach used traditionally by the STEM field.
In doing so, this curriculum can spark innovation within learners to explore new viewpoints.

Beyond these projects, Mona has tried to maintain a balanced lifestyle by pursuing various hobbies and interests that she is passionate about. For example, Mona has a great love of knitting. She has created her own designs and products for various items such as scarves and bags that are available on her website, *Knits by Mona*. Furthermore, she has created a blog called Banana Days, a name that was inspired by her childhood dislike of bananas. The blog highlights various moments in her life as a blind, female, Muslim scientist through jokes, stories, and thoughts. Besides her blog, she has other day-to-day interests. As implied by PTC, Mona has a great love for travelling because it gives her the opportunity to embrace new opportunities. She is an avid listener of audio books, which includes Sherlock Holmes and Harry Potter. Mona also does martial arts, tandem biking, and rock climbing to stay active. All in all,

Mona is an incredible and multifaceted individual who has pursued many interests and has achieved many things.

Space Travels and Mission AstroAccess

Mona's achievements do not end there. Mona has made a giant leap for mankind by being part of experiments involving space travel. With a focus on accessibility for the visually impaired, Mona has taken part in a series of flights that have replicated conditions in space as an Astro Access ambassador. Mona has provided interesting insights on how the physical environment aboard space vessels can be modified such that all space travellers, regardless of disability, can travel to space.

Mona's curiosity regarding space started even before she became an Astro Access ambassador. Her interest was first sparked during the time when rich billionaires such as Jeff Bezos were going to space. While she also really wanted to go, she never thought she would get the opportunity to go. Mona was in for a surprise very shortly after this thought. As stated by Mona herself, "Two weeks [after having the thought to go to space], I kid you not, I got a call from Dr. Sheri Wells-Jensen! She was like: Would you like to experience ZERO GRAVITY!?!" Mona was thrilled to be offered the chance to be part of this project. After some application procedures, she got the news that she would be able to experience zero gravity. Mona was one of the four blind/low visual individuals, along with two deaf individuals and six mobility-impaired individuals on the flight. Her hope was to demonstrate that solutions exist to overcome what appear to be barriers to individuals with disabilities.

The first flight occurred on 17th October, 2021 in Los Angeles, near Long Beach. As described by Mona, "It was a nice and lovely day. I remember it…. it was sunny and very exciting." The Astro Access ambassadors were given the recommendation to eat anti-motion medications, which have drowsiness as a potential side effect, to prepare for the flight. However, Mona refused because "[she] refused to be drowsy on the coolest day of [her] life." Before the flight, everyone came together to figure out the various experiments to run during this flight. Along with having various devices for testing, Mona had a small cane that she named the "space cane," which she was going to use to help her. Then, they all went up on the flight.

Obtaining zero gravity was done through a parabolic flight, which involves having a plane go up and down in parabolas. More specifically, zero gravity is experienced by the passengers when the plane moves downwards, from the top of the parabola, at a specific angle. The flight done with the Astro Access ambassadors involved 15 parabolas: two replicated Martian gravity, the next two were lunar gravity, and then the rest were of zero gravity. Mona was glad to have Martian gravity first because she jumped up in excitement during the first parabola, something she was warned not to do, and accidentally hit the ceiling with her head! During the first few parabolas, Mona realised that she needed to calm down to prevent that from happening again. After that, lunar gravity came in. This part of the flight was incredibly amazing to Mona because: "It was like the best trampoline jump." Then came the part of the flight that Mona was most excited about: experiencing zero gravity. Mona remembers telling herself that this would be her first ever moment that she would be able to experience zero gravity. She would never be able to relive that moment because you can never have a second first. When it came, she started to float and was amazed at the experience. As Mona describes, this was "one of the coolest experiences of [her] life" because it was the one time in life that she was "truly untethered from everything else."

Mona has since participated in two more flights to gain a better understanding of how to modify spacecraft to accommodate visually impaired individuals. Astro Access collaborated with the Aurelia Institute and MIT to give Mona this opportunity. During these two flights, Mona ran an experiment where she video taped herself and narrated where she was during the flight. This data gave an indication of how accurate Mona was in deducing her location. She learned about the importance of tactile sensation for determining location. If she was not touching anything, then she did not know where she was. But, if she was able to touch anything, she could identify her location with ease. On these flights, Mona also did some experiments on tactile modifications. The sides of the plane were covered with different textures to give an indication of which side of the plane was which and more.

These three flights have made Mona the most experienced blind zero gravity researcher, an extremely impressive accomplishment that Mona is proud of. Mona gained several insights through this experience. Firstly, when having to go back to her seat, finding her spot was much easier than what was originally thought. Prior to her flights, many individuals were worried that Mona would not be able to figure out where to go, which she proved as false. Secondly, the conditions in the plane made it very loud. Mona lost her auditory usage, meaning that it was not as helpful to navigate by sound. This could potentially disorient blind individuals and, thereby, would require an increased use of tactile sensation for the visually impaired. Lastly, 20 seconds is much shorter than you can imagine. While conceptually understandable, Mona realised this because zero-gravity was only experienced for 20 seconds before passengers were required to return to their seats. These insights will be incredibly helpful in the future.

Mona has full confidence that in the future visually impaired individuals can be sent to space. She even believes that they could be an asset. For example, there was a circumstance where smoke impaired the visual capabilities of astronauts on the International Space Station (ISS). This situation had a disorienting effect on the passengers because no one was trained to not use their eyesight. However, if a blind astronaut was present on the crew, they would be able to navigate through this situation with a greater degree of ease because they were accustomed to having a lack of sight. For this reason and more, visually impaired individuals can be extremely beneficial during flights to space.

Conclusion

In a time where the foundations of space travel are being laid down, conversations about the accessibility of space crafts and life in space are essential to ensure those from different backgrounds will be able to travel to space. The experiments conducted by Astro Access Ambassadors, such as Mona, show the first steps in this process. They demonstrate that those with disabilities are just as capable of space travel as long as simple considerations, such as having various textures on the wall for blind people or flashing lights for deaf individuals, are taken into account for them. Overall, Mona Minkara's story is truly inspirational, and her insights show that visually impaired individuals should not be underestimated because they are more than capable of flying to space and achieving amazing things.

The information is this chapter is sourced from a personal interview with Mona Minkara and through her website (https://monaminkara.com/)

Chapter 5: Accessible spacecraft making way for an accessible earth, from interview with Sawyer Rosenstein

By Angela Kazmierczak

Many people fantasize about becoming the next Daniel Craig, Djimon Hounson, or Kate Winslet. Young Sawyer Rosenstein was headed in that direction. Working as a professional child actor in New York City—the city of colossal skyscrapers, baked pretzels, and the Yankee stadium—Rosenstein performed in a series of commercials, jingles, voiceovers, and Macy's Thanksgiving parades. But, in 2006, at the age of 12, things would dramatically change for him. While at his New Jersey middle school, a bully ambushed him, striking Rosenstein in the face. Two days later, Rosenstein awoke paralyzed from the waist down, making him a T10-12 paraplegic. Now immobile and in need of accessible options, Rosenstein attended a local space camp called the Challenger Center, where he and other campers learned about aviation, rocketry, and robotics. On a whim, Rosenstein "became the camper that never left." For the next 12 years, Rosenstein worked at the space camp and taught kids about simulated space missions. The more he discovered and taught kids about space, the more he felt drawn to space reporting.

Eventually, Rosenstein went on to become the radio host of "Talking Space" and a space reporter who frequently attended launches from the grounds. Whenever a space shuttle lifted off though, he looked longingly at the sky for the day it would be his turn. The dream felt like an ulterior reality, separated as far as the Earendel, the furthest morning star the Hubble Telescope ever observed (Hickey, 2022). He knew his paralysis impeded his chances at space flight, making him completely disregard the idea. But like many movie characters, his peripeteia would change. Mission: AstroAccess, a project devoted to disability inclusion, selected Rosenstein as an ambassador, and he would, in much disbelief, take his spin at a zero-gravity flight with 11 other disabled persons. His mission narrowed in on three objectives: to show he could get from one point to another, hold his position, and control where his legs went when floating. Ultimately, his success, his ability to perform these tasks in a weightless environment, could revolutionize space inclusion, which more than likely lingered in his mind in the days leading to the flight.

A year following his flight, he has gathered various sentiments from his 15 parabolas, especially in terms of design and accessibility. What's most striking is the ambassador claims that with declining spaceflight costs and with Mission: AstroAccess' accessibility designs underway, it opens those disabled to the possibility of space exploration and accessibility on earth.

"We're at the perfect time in space flight for all these things to be happening. This is essentially the dawn of the new age of commercial space, where commercial space is becoming more readily available, it's becoming cheaper," said Rosenstein.

He isn't making outlandish claims about cheapening costs either. When we look back in time from 1961 to 1972, after President John F. Kennedy announced the nation's goal to land on the moon, NASA spent $28 billion on the Apollo Program (Carter, 2020; NASA, 2019). The Apollo program consisted of 11 space flights and six landings on the moon and aimed to "develop human capacity to work in the lunar environment" (NASA, p. 1). As many recount, one of the flights included the infamous Neil Armstrong and Edwin "Buzz" Aldrin, the first Americans to walk on the moon and sink a flag into the moon's surface—called the "lunar regolith" (Wild, 2019). This program tallies $283 billion today (Carter, para. 6).

Currently, NASA projects that the cost of the 2024 Artemis mission, which includes a lunar landing of the first woman and person of color, is $28 billion. That means the Artemis mission costs a tenth of the Apollo program (Carter, 2020). Then, in February of 2022, 90-minute space flights on Virgin Galactic sold for $450,000 (Molina, 2022). Space tourism isn't as far-fetched as during the release of Star Trek and Star Wars fantasy films. Private companies are materializing new heights in space exploration.

According to Chow (2022), the growth of these private space companies, "lower costs to launch into space, and the availability of smaller, cheaper components to build satellites and other spacecraft" (para. 9). He links these advancements to spaceflight freeing from government dominance (para. 9). In other words, newly emerging private companies, such as SpaceX or Rocket Lab, create a competitive market, ultimately lowering space travel costs. That makes space tourism more obtainable and luring, especially to the wealthy. Space strategist Josef Koller claims it leaves room for innovation too. Furthermore, commercial flight opens a seat to whoever, not just NASA astronauts (Grush, 2021). Rosenstein urges, however: "Rather than thinking of accessibility as an afterthought, this is the time where it can be incorporated into these new designs." Before 2021's Mission: AstroAccess flight, only one person with a disability had ever completed a zero-gravity mission.

That person was none other than physicist and cosmologist Stephen Hawking. In 2007, Hawking, who suffered from Amyotrophic Lateral Sclerosis (ALS), a disease degenerating the motor neurons in the brain, experienced four minutes of weightlessness. In interviews with Hawkins, he described it as a "sweet relief from the bondage of a daily life immobilized by a debilitating and irreversible neuromuscular disorder" (New Scientist, 2007, para. 6). From flying, Hawkins hoped "the experience [would] lead to a suborbital spaceflight aboard a new passenger service" (para. 14). Given his demobilizing disease and the doubts of others, Hawkins longed to show that "everybody can participate in this kind of activity" (para. 11).

As revealed in his response, Hawkins knew that space exploration was reserved for a minute group of people. From 1957 to 2001, about 600 people flew to space (Roulette, 2021). When NASA began selecting astronauts in 1959, astronauts were required to be shorter than 5' 11"—due to limited cabin space—and carry a doctorate in medicine, natural sciences, or engineering. The requirements have since changed for astronauts—possess a master's degree in STEM-related programs, gain two years of relevant experience or 1,000 hours of pilot-in-command time, pass the astronaut physical, and be an American citizen (Deiss, 2020). Today, not much has changed as NASA candidates require perfect health, and any major disabilities will disqualify them. However, applicants no longer need 20/20 vision but can undergo eye surgery (Grush, 2021). Meanwhile, the Federal Aviation Administration (FAA), which revised its commercial flight criteria in 2021, requires that the crew launch to at least 50 miles and "demonstrate activities during the flight that were essential to human safety" (Froust, 2021, para. 3). The FAA established the rules to "promote commercial space transportation and oversee its safety" (para. 13).

After these revisements in criteria for commerical flights, in 2021, reporter Rosenstein and 11 other AstroAccess disabled ambassadors embarked on a weightless flight to make space flight history. Instead of one disabled member, an entire crew would carry out a series of missions. Now, Rosenstein hopes that following the flight, space inclusivity will continue to evolve and be incorporated into future space flight designs.

"The hope is that the work done from this [Flight One] will lead to allowing people with disabilities to fly on those flights or fly to space and that as these companies are designing spacecraft, it won't be an afterthought," he said.

"The more we do with these flights, hopefully with these things we find out, they'll be able to be incorporated into these designs. And I can say that at least with what I had with flight one, that some of these changes they can make are so simple," Rosenstein said.

In the initial planning phase, Rosenstein vocalized concern for his legs flying apart since he doesn't have control over them. After some collaborative planning, the group used a Velcro strap to hold his legs together. Needless to say, it worked; it didn't require a major overhaul to be designed, as many would assume. From this design, along with others, like placing pockets and zippers on flight suits pertinent to the ambassador's needs, he hopes that people will see how simple modifications are in these circumstances and that they can be easily incorporated.

However, Rosenstein strongly believes the flights are about more than creating space equality and accessibility.

"As much as [Flight One] was about creating accessibility in space, space flight, and spacecraft, a lot of it is honestly just to help design for accessibility here on earth because so many times people claim things are accessible and they're not, or something has to be retrofitted to be accessible," said Rosenstein.

Many online articles vocalize this sentiment too. In an article by Jones (2019), several disabled persons voiced their laments over a lack of accessible options. Some explained that several places failed to install accessible tools, and many businesses that appeared to be accessible weren't. Others mentioned how many ramps are too steep for wheelchairs, and bumps at the bottom of ramps create issues since some disabled persons cannot lift their walkers over them. In many discussions, buildings' entrances marked where accessibility ended, and washrooms were far too much a feat. Essentially, stalls were too narrow; depending on how doors opened and closed, a person in a wheelchair was trapped inside or outside the stall (p. 1).

As suggested by the Accessibility for Ontarians with Disabilities Act (2019):

People who own or operate organizations can welcome more visitors or customers when they recognize, remove, and prevent barriers. Identifying a barrier means knowing that a barrier exists. For instance, a building owner recognizes a barrier when they realize that heavy doors limit people's access to the building. (para. 3)

Generally, AODA, which helps mandate accessibility standards in the province, identifies five barriers to watch for: physical or architectural barriers, informational or communicational barriers, technological barriers, organizational barriers, and attitudinal barriers (Kovac, para. 5). AODA emphasizes the importance of creating accessible environments as it provides a more welcoming family environment, helps businesses gain more clients and customers, and it allows employees to hire those with disabilities (para. 4).

"The families, friends, neighbors, and colleagues of people with disabilities may want to bring their business to accessible companies. Furthermore, people without disabilities may find accessible features, from widened aisles to welcoming staff, useful or enjoyable," said Kovac on the AODA website.

As mentioned earlier, Rosenstein hopes these flights and Zero-G tests lead to a more accessible earth. But to materialize that reality and inch ever closer, he and the Astro team are working to prepare the Flight 2 crew and evolve their initial designs. Currently, the team is working on suit modifications and finding ways to keep things in place—something akin to foot holds but suitable for those who cannot use their feet. If the crew successfully finds this modification, it will allow ambassadors to stay in place and use their hands freely.

Rosenstein is optimistic that "something we design that can help keep us stationary in space is something that can be used to help us here back on earth or some of these designs or tests that we do on Zero-G can help change accessibility on earth as well," he said.

"[Astro is] working on things like that."

"I'm very happy as a space reporter, being there on the ground, talking to the people going into space, watching the rockets launch, knowing there's slim to no chance of me doing it." Rosenstein continues, "but knowing there are people out there working on ways to make this accessible and are actually trying to get people with disabilities at least into a Zero-Gravity environment to practice, prepare, and all these companies allow for people with disabilities to fly, it changed my whole perspective."

"I know from my work that I proved in my first flight that it can be done—that 14 out of 15 times I made it back to the correct spot, in a safe position in time for what would've been a so-called re-entry, but in our case, it was just the end of the parabola," Rosenstein said.

The Mission: AstroAccess Flight 2 lifts off November 19, 2022, from Fort Lauderdale, Florida. The organization now accepts international applications, but applications for the second flight are currently closed.

References

Carter, J. (2020, September 23). 8 reasons why NASA's $28 billion moon return is the bargain of

the century. *Forbes*. Retrieved from https://www.nbcnews.com/science/space-

launch-costs-growing-business-industry-rcna23488

Chow, D. (2022, April 8). To cheaply go: How falling launch costs fuelled a thriving economy in

orbit. *NBC News Science*. Retrieved from https://www.nbcnews.com/science/space/

-launch-costs-growing-business-industry-rcna23488

Deiss, H. (2022, January 14). *Astronaut requirements*. National Aeronautics and Space

Administration. Retrieved from https://www.nasa.gov/audience/forstudents/postsecondary/features/F_Astronaut_Requirements.html

Foust, J. (2021, July 21). FAA revises criteria for commercial astronaut wings. *Space News*. Retrieved from https://spacenews.com/faa-revises-criteria-for-commercial-astronaut-wings/

Grush, L. (2021, October 20). The mission to break barriers to space travel for people with disabilities. *The Verge*. Retrieved from https://www.theverge.com/2021/10/20/2273433/mission-astro-access-disability-zero-g-flight-space-travel

Hickey, J. (2022, April 5). NASA finds Earendel, the farthest star. *Skywatch 16*. Retrieved from https://www.wnep.com/article/weather/skywatch-16/farthest-star-in-space-skywatch-16-hubble-space-telescope-earendel-nasa/523-eae7a0bb-d024-4158-be16-96a04bae569d

Jones, H. M. (2019, September 27). My disability taught me that the world is rarely accessible.

Healthline. Retrieved from https://www.healthline.com/health/my-disability-taught-me-

that-the-world-isnt-truly-accessible-at-all#1

Kovac, L. (2018, October 2). *What is the AODA?* Accessibility for Ontarians with Disabilities

Act. Retrieved from https://aoda.ca/what-is-the-aoda/

Molina, B. (2022, February 15). How much is a seat on Virgin Galactic? $450,000. Here's what

each trip includes. *USA Today*. Retrieved from https://www.usatoday.com/story/tech/202

2/02/15/virgin-galactic-tickets-space-trip/6795121001/

New Scientist & Reuters. (2007, April 26). Stephen Hawking gets taste of zero gravity. *New*

Scientist. Retrieved from https://www.newscientist.com/article/dn11730-stephen-

hawking-gets-taste-of-zero-gravity/

Roulette, J. (2021, November 10). More than 600 beings have now been to space. *The New York*

Times. Retrieved from https://www.nytimes.com/2021/11/10/

science/600-astronauts-space.html

Wild, F. (2019, July 18). *What was the Apollo program?* National Aeronautics and Space Administration. Retrieved from https://www.nasa.gov/audience/forstudents/5-8/features/nasa-knows/what-was-apollo-program-58.html

Chapter 6: Disability and need for inclusivity on space missions

Manahil Jawad

Approximately one billion individuals worldwide experience some form of disability. Individuals with disabilities include people with physical, intellectual, sensory impairments, and psychosocial impairments. However, various forms of disabilities are not always physically apparent. In addition, environmental and societal barriers hinder the inclusion and effective participation of individuals with disabilities on an equal basis for others (Xang, n.d.).

Research shows that various factors such as an aging population, an increasing number of injuries resulting from natural disasters and longer life expectancy, the number of people with disabilities in coming decades are expected to increase. Individuals with disabilities face challenges in Science, Technology, Engineering and Mathematics (STEM). Many barriers to using or accessing knowledge and resources avert the participation of persons with disabilities in research and activities essential for advancement in the field (Xang, n.d.).
As a society, we are responsible for being more inclusive and equitable through collective efforts. An organization that aims to build a more inclusive space in Astro research is the United Nations office of outer space affairs (UNOOSA). Through its disability inclusion strategy and Space for Persons with Disabilities, the project aims to engage persons

with disabilities in space science as physical disabilities have until now been avoided in space (Wickramanayake, n.d.). The project enhances prospects for individuals with disabilities to progress into careers in STEM, besides engaging decision makers to assist and facilitate initiatives targeting inclusivity in space science. A collective effort from a pool of best-qualified persons is required for space exploration; an effective way to do it is by including more people of different ages, genders and backgrounds, including people with physical disabilities. Space can contribute in various ways to achieving disability inclusion and can have transformational effects on persons with disabilities (Wickramanayake, n.d.).

The UN convention on the rights of persons with disabilities (CRPD) recognizes the right of persons with disabilities and aligns with the UN disability inclusion strategy. The vision of UNOOSA's space for persons with disabilities project is to promote sustainable development and an equitable and inclusive space by mainstreaming the rights of persons with disabilities. In addition, partnerships enhance prospects for persons with disabilities to advance their education and careers in space. To ensure the inclusion of individuals with disabilities, a systematic and integrated approach in internal, and external operations and programming is required.

UNOOSA, building on the vision of achieving sustainable and transformative progress on disability inclusion in space, has adopted a two-pronged approach. One is mainstreaming disability in its internal processes and broader work considering disability-associated perspectives. The second is the development of disability-specific programs through meaningful and informed involvement of individuals with disabilities. Sonification, a tool for scientific research and disability inclusion in space are the two activities undertaken by UNOOSA for which consultation is in progress. UNOOSA invites all stakeholders in developing and developed countries to share projects, programmes, policies, technologies, practices, experiences, and lessons that promote inclusive and accessible space science education and progression. It encourages disability inclusion and accessibility in space science education and profession. Information shared and obtained will lead to developing a research report encompassing taking stock of disability inclusion in space globally and providing insights on good international practices (Xang, n.d.).

NASA ((National Aeronautics and Space Administration) is an independent agency of the US government. It still follows the prerequisite of the right stuff and tough by disqualifying individuals with known physical disabilities from spaceflight, thus keeping them ground-bound. NASA's current requirements for astronaut applicants include being a US citizen, holding a master's degree in a STEM field, having completed two years of related professional experience and being able to pass long-duration flight astronaut physical. According to NASA, each crew member must be free of medical conditions that would impair the ability of a person to participate in space flight.

Though in the late 1950s/in the 1960s, NASA conducted a study in which 11 deaf men participated, however; the purpose was to understand the effects of prolonged weightlessness on the human body. Due to vestibular system differences in some deaf people, no adverse physical effects were reported, and they were immune to motion sickness compared to their non-deaf counterparts. The experiment by NASA proved that deaf space flight participants are more adaptable to foreign gravitational environments. However, even then, NASA did not send any deaf astronauts to space. Rather NASA bars persons with mobility-related disabilities and those who are blind or deaf.

However, NASA investigated the feasibility of sending people with disabilities safely into space and returning them to Earth which is a positive step regarding the inclusion of disabilities in space missions. The evaluation is known as the Parastronaut Feasibility Foundational Research Study, issued in November 2021 by the Potomac Institute for

Policy Studies of Arlington, Virginia. The study was done for NASA's office of the Chief health medical officer. They undertook it after consultation with medical experts, other organizations, and military and industry leaders besides subject matter experts, and former astronauts. In this study, para astronauts are defined as individuals with certain physical disabilities, such as lower leg deficiencies, short stature and differences in leg length.

The appraisal makes many recommendations and suggestions, including revising medical standards for selecting astronauts and using parabolic aircraft flights to show para astronaut proof of principle. According to Alyssa Adcock, a Potomac Institute research fellow who spearheaded the report, "I do see the para astronaut study as an initial step towards a larger endeavour, an initial starting point." Adcock views the study "as the first step towards inclusivity and a much larger way that we view human spaceflight and access to human spaceflight."

According to performer NASA chief and astronaut Charles Bolden, a senior fellow at the Potomac Institute, "NASA should be open to doing as much research as possible to help the private sector understand how best to fully integrate less than fully physically capable people into a crew." He added, "I do believe that there are very few physical limitations to successfully flying in space. A para astronaut can be an incredible crew member contributor." Several study data points suggest that para astronauts may become a bigger part of the spaceflight picture in the future (David & Ali, 2021).

Human spaceflight is in the midst of a major transformation as the rise of commercial spaceflight has challenged the conventional definition of an astronaut. Now it is no more just NASA's game as in the last few decades, various private companies have sprung up to send humans to a different part of space. Companies like Virgin Galactic and Blue Origin have developed suborbital vehicles designed to carry paying customers to the edge of space and back so that they can experience a short glimpse of Earth from above.

SpaceX is a company which has started flying people to low earth orbit on its new crew Dragon spacecraft. Recently SpaceX undertook its Inspiration4 mission in which the company flew a crew of 4 civilians to orbit, the first-ever human spaceflight to orbit Earth with only private citizens on board. In September 2021, these four crew members circled planet earth for three days on a SpaceX crew dragon capsule. The significance of this mission was the inclusion of Hayley Arceneaux, a physician assistant at St Jude children's research hospital, a pediatric cancer survivor, who underwent chemotherapy and had surgery to replace some of her leg bones with prosthetics. With an internal prosthesis in her leg, something that would have disqualified her from flying as a NASA astronaut. Although SpaceX sent the first person with a prosthesis to space, she was not the first person as Stephen Hawking in, 2007 went on a parabolic flight and described the experience as true freedom (Grush, 2021).

In early 2021, the European Space Agency (ESA) announced its "Parastronaut Feasibility Project," which is centred on the inclusion of persons with a physical disability while still ensuring that a mission is productive and safe. ESA is looking for cognitively, psychologically, technically, and professionally qualified individuals to be astronauts but have physical disabilities. This would usually prevent them from being selected because of the requirements of using current space hardware. For the project, ESA is recruiting a qualified individual with all qualifications to become an astronaut. The individual must have one of three physical conditions/disabilities: lower limb deficiency (due to amputation or congenital limb deficiency that is single or double foot deficiency through the ankle or single or double leg deficiency below the knee), a pronounced leg length difference or short stature (defined as under 130 centimetres, or about four feet, three inches).

The pilot aspect of the para astronaut feasibility project is inclusiveness. ESA intends to select and fly an astronaut with a physical disability. There is a great value in diversity, and including people with special needs also means benefiting from their extraordinary experience, ability to adapt to difficult environments, and point of view. To learn about the ESA project and to explore the challenges and opportunities in this emerging field, with the support of ESA in March 2021, a webinar, "Pushing Frontiers: Human Spaceflight and Disability," was organized by the UNOOSA. For the ESA project, launching a first physically disabled astronaut into space, by January 2022, the agency had narrowed 22,000+ applications down to below 1,400 for its 4- to 6-person program—and 29 of those remaining applicants have a physical disability. With increasing shifts of space flights to private companies, more opportunities for expanded access to space may exist ("Para astronaut feasibility project").

SciAccess announced its program Mission AstroAcess with the generous support of the Whitesides Foundation and through the Zero Gravity Corporation (ZERO-G). As the first step in the progression toward flying a diverse range of people to space, AstroAccess is a project promoting disability inclusion in space exploration. It was planned to launch a group of disabled scientists, veterans, students, athletes, and artists on historic parabolic flights. The purpose of the parabolic flight was to experience weightlessness and carry out lunar gravity, Martian gravity, and zero gravity observations and experiments. In addition, it investigates how the physical environment in space vessels should be modified so all astronauts and explorers, regardless of their limitations and disabilities on Earth, can live, work, and thrive in space ("Astroaccess", "Sci access").

Historic parabolic flight took off from Long Beach on Oct 17, 2021, with a group of veterans, disabled scientists, students, athletes and artists. They were launched into a zero-gravity environment as a first step toward understanding what is needed to make space inclusive for all. Dr. Erik Viirre, served as medical/flight operations lead for the AstroAccess flight ensuring a safe environment for all 12 ActroAccess

Ambassadors and their partners abroad. According to him, "The whole point of this project is to demonstrate that people with disabilities can fly safely into space".

Inclusive space exploration was the common goal of the AstroAccess project led by a group of scientists, engineers, and social workers. 26% of the population has a US disability, yet people with disabilities make up only 8.4% of the country's employed scientists and engineers. AstroAccess wants to make STEM and space accessible to this large portion of the population. For this first microgravity flight, 12 AstroAccess Ambassadors were selected, including four blind or low-vision Ambassadors, two deaf or hard-of-hearing Ambassadors, and six Ambassadors with mobility disabilities. All had to carry out various tasks in the weightless environment. including safety and operational tasks. They also investigated how American Sign Language will be impacted by microgravity. On Oct 17, a plane equipped with a special padded section flew up to an altitude of around 32,000 feet and then began a rapid descent at about 4 miles per second (Crowell, 2021). This was not the first time someone with a disability experienced microgravity. Stephen Hawking 2007 travelled on a Zero-G flight. Hawking described experiencing "true freedom ... I was Superman for those few minutes". Although Hawking died in 2018, the goal of sending disabled astronauts did not die with him. One of the 12 Ambassadors was Mona Minkara, a Northeastern University bioengineer who leads a laboratory focused pulmonary research using applying computational modelling. She travelled with 11 other individuals with mobility, vision or hearing disabilities on a parabolic flight with the Zero Gravity Corporation. The mission, which allowed participants to feel weightless but did not reach space, was an initiative dedicated to "advancing disability inclusion in space" (Ufberg, 2022). AstroAccess has partnered with the Aurelia Institute to promote disability inclusion in space. Horizon 2022 zero gravity flight took place on May 22, led by Aurelia. Including ambassadors for AstroAccess,

25 crew participated from various organizations. The 90-minute mission simulated space flight with 20 parabolas of lunar, Martian, and zero gravity that lasted about 20 seconds each. Participants focused on specific new tests and experiments as each crew member on the Horizon flight had a research goal, art project and task o complete within microgravity. Using only handholds, Centra "Ce-Ce" Mazyck, a wheelchair user, navigated the cabin. Mona Minkara got oriented without sight and used textured surfaces (velcro and corduroy) on the cabin's walls. Apurva Varia tested LED lights that non-verbally signalled deaf flyers to prepare for zero gravity. After the AstroAccess flight in October 2021 and the flight in May 2022, to further evaluate and promote disability inclusion in space, the next flight is scheduled on Nov 19, 2022, with a crew of new and repeat ambassadors ("Making Space Travel").

References

Xang. (n.d.). *United NationsOffice for Outer Space Affairs*. Space4People with Disabilities. Retrieved September 2, 2022, from https://www.unoosa.org/oosa/en/ourwork/space4personswithdisabilites/index.html

Wickramanayake, R. (n.d.). *United NationsOffice for Outer Space Affairs*. Space4Persons with Disabilities. Retrieved September 2, 2022, from https://www.unoosa.org/oosa/en/ourwork/space4personswithdisabilites/space4persons-with-disabilities.html

David, L. (2021, December 31). *Equal Access to Space: New Study investigates how to get more 'Parastronauts' aloft*. Space.com. Retrieved September 2, 2022, from https://www.space.com/inclusive-human-spaceflight-parastronaut-study

Ali, S. (2021, December 13). *This space company wants to help people with disabilities become astronauts*. The Hill. Retrieved

September 2, 2022, from https://thehill.com/changing-america/respect/accessibility/585335-this-space-company-wants-to-help-people-with/

Grush, L. (2021, October 20). *The mission to break barriers to space travel for people with disabilities*. The Verge. Retrieved September 2, 2022, from https://www.theverge.com/2021/10/20/22734331/mission-astro-access-disability-zero-g-flight-space-travel

Parastronaut feasibility project. ESA. (n.d.). Retrieved September 2, 2022, from https://www.esa.int/About_Us/Careers_at_ESA/ESA_Astronaut_Selection/Parastronaut_feasibility_project

AstroAccess - Crunchbase Company Profile & Funding. Crunchbase. (n.d.). Retrieved September 2, 2022, from https://www.crunchbase.com/organization/astroaccess

Home. SciAccess. (2022, March 15). Retrieved September 2, 2022, from https://sciaccess.org/

Making space travel inclusive for all. Making Space Travel Inclusive for All. (2021, October 28). Retrieved September 2, 2022, from https://ucsdnews.ucsd.edu/feature/making-space-travel-inclusive-for-all

Crowell, R. (2021, October 20). *Disabled astronauts blaze new space trails*. Scientific American. Retrieved September 2, 2022, from https://www.scientificamerican.com/article/disabled-astronauts-blaze-new-space-trails/

Ufberg, M. (2022, June 23). *How astroaccess plans to make space more accessible*. Fast Company. Retrieved September 2, 2022, from https://www.fastcompany.com/90764012/how-astroaccess-plans-to-make-space-more-accessible

Chapter 7: Flight ops and the future, Dr. Jamie Molaro

Francis Fernandes

Mission AstroAccess (MAA) has gained international recognition as a project dedicated to advocate and investigate people with disabilities in space through parabolic flights (Mission Astro Access, 2022). To date, it has spearheaded the completion of the first parabolic flight that included a diverse participant-group, many of whom had disabilities (Mission Astro Access, 2022).

The purpose of MAA is intended to be far greater than an effort to enhance the diversity of individuals involved in spaceflight – rather, the initiative aims to empirically observe and investigate what unique insights can be learned from involving people with disabilities in zero-gravity environments (Planetary Science Institute, 2022). Such insights are intended to improve accessibility design which may present positive implications for existing space-flight operations and further enable persons-with-disabilities in space-flight activities (Planetary Science Institute, 2022).

To gauge a deeper understanding of MAA's activities, current progress, future directions and personal outlooks – AIC had the opportunity to interview and write on a number of MAA personnel including the project leads, organizing team and flight crew. Dr. Jamie Molaro is the current flight operations and research & publication lead for MAA. The aims of the interview were to get a candid view on her professional work, motivation to participate in MAA, the progress of MAA, and what to expect in the future.

In brief, what are some of your current roles and responsibilities, in terms of research and professional affiliations?
"Yeah, I mean, I'm involved in the number of projects. Firstly, I am a research scientist with the Planetary Science Institute. Geographically, I work from Southern California, and I have an office at the Jet Propulsion Laboratory, which is the NASA Center here – so I'm affiliated sort of with both places.
In particular, my research focuses on physical weathering processes and ways that, like rocky and icy landscapes and surfaces, evolve overtime. I also look into rock fracturing as well as the evolution of ice – in essence its about understanding how landscapes and the solar system change over time.
I am a member of the science team of the Osiris Rex Mission, which is the asteroid sample return mission – there will be an extended mission to another asteroid, which is also exciting."

What about some of your personal interests, I had read keenly about your interest in the arts as well as your advocacy work?
"Yes ! I do a lot of art myself.
I am an artist and I create data-driven works that use spacecraft data to create the art and I teach workshops now about doing this.
I've been doing that this year and I do a lot of art shows promoting and displaying this type of art as a different way of engaging with the public and with other communities about the kinds of work and research that we're doing.
And on the disability side, so I am the director of small social and peer networking group called DIAS or Disabled for Accessibility & Space. We started that last year as a place for space professionals/space-related professionals who've had disabilities or chronic illnesses to come

together, network, get advice and support. And it was through DIAS that I got connected with Mission Astro Access (MAA).
That's how I ended up at MAA. I helped with the flight last year as a colleague of the Flight Operations Committee and this year I will act as the lead of flight operations."

As the lead of flight operations, what are you looking to investigate in terms of disability and space flight?
"As the lead of flight operations, one of my goals is to the team develop the experiments and the research that we're trying to conduct on the parabolic flight. As a researcher, my primary goal is to enable the team and the flight crews themselves to prepare for what can we actually learn from doing this experiment? Because it's really not about just putting people on a plane. It's about actually getting substantive.
Meaningful learning outcomes from such experiments can feed into things like accessible design and spacecrafts, flight suits designs and other types of things like that.I suppose I have my hands and a lot of projects at the moment, but MAA has been one of the big ones really over the last several months."

It's apparent that your professional work, collaborations, and affiliations are profound based on the project and teams you are working with. Additionally, you have taken expanded your interest in arts through creating works and educating your peers. Amidst all this, you have managed to start the DIAS group and now lead the flight ops for MAA. Where did this interest on working with people with disabilities start – and what keeps you going?
"That's a good question. For me starting DAIS was personal.
I would say I myself am disabled – I have a connective tissue disorder that affects my joints. I was unaware of this as I was younger but has gotten progressively worse and played a bigger role in my life as I have grown older. I really started having problems with it during Graduate

61

School and then over the last several years.

With that, there is a process you go through when you're coming into something like this and coming in terms with how much this really does affect my life a lot. I had to change my life in significant ways because of this. And like, does that mean I'm disabled? Like, what does it mean to be disabled? Am I even allowed to use that word? Everybody has a different relationship with that word. Some people prefer the term, and some people don't.

I really had to figure out a lot of things about how to deal with that. While also trying to get through grad school and trying to start my career and learning how to do things like; how do I ask for accommodations from my workplace? Am I even allowed to ask for accommodations? Will they let me? What kind of accommodations are even available for somebody like me?

I am a very assertive and confident person and I'm good at advocating for myself, but not everyone necessarily is. There can be a cost to that, to somebody's career, depending on the context. There is a risk that you can be discriminated against in one way or another Because of that, I just thought that others shouldn't have to go through process of figuring this out alone.

There's no reason why we shouldn't be able to support each other and help each other figure out how to do those things. So really the goal of DIAS was to bring people together and try and help others go through what I did, but maybe a little bit easier and with some more support.

I think disability isn't something that a lot of people in society really think that much about, to be honest, until you have one or you know somebody who has one and you get a little bit of experience with it. I certainly didn't before, and now I do.

And with that, I just feel like I want to help others make that journey – Astro access thing was just sort of an extended project on top of that."

Learning about the challenges that you encountered when realizing and navigating your disability in relation to your everyday-life/ career and using that as the basis of your advocacy effort and MAA contribution is truly compelling. What I also find truly fascinating is this focus of disability beyond an initiative of inclusion. Rather then enhancing the diversity and enabling inclusion of those who can pursue space travel, there really seems to be an articulate investigation of disability in the space environment – what are your thought on this?

"You're absolutely right that we have tried to make the project have that focus.

There's a common problem in the way that disabled people can often be depicted in media or news stories. That like 'Oh, there's this inspiring story of somebody overcoming the fact that they don't have legs by climbing Mount Everest or whatever'.

And it doesn't change, of course, that is inspiring, but it's not inspiring in the way that everybody thinks that it is. I mean that's not the right way of saying it.

The thing is that it shouldn't have to be inspiring because we should have a society where, like people are just supported in getting the accommodations they need to function, you know? So climbing Mount Everest is a little bit of a hyperbolic example, of course.

If we had basic disability accommodations everywhere in our physical environment that like everybody could function normally – you know *"normally"*.

Our goal with the flights is not just to give everybody an inspiring story that shows 'oh yeah, disabled people are capable'. We know they're capable because we are them and we're independent and we live our daily lives every single day. However, this doesn't change the fact that the world is not designed for many of us in a lot of different ways, not just the physical environment, but also the cultural environment and in social aspects as well.

Ultimately, the goal is to get something that is meaningful out of what we're doing that can change the way that things are done.

There's a cost to flying an airplane – not just a financial cost but also an environmental cost. Additionally, there's a cost of time and all the funds that accumulated donated to this project to make this happen.

That being said, we're not just in it for a story, we're in it to really to learn something.

There's a few of us on the team in particular who really highly focus on that. And because I am a researcher so the goal is always for me; What can I learn from what I'm observing and what I'm doing?

We're really trying to focus on research around things like; how could we design a physical environment that is more accessible to people who have lower limbs? How do you design a handhold for somebody to anchor themselves in zero gravity? If they don't have a hand what kinds of physical environments can we create/modify?

Physical environments can include a flight suit, a tool that's being used. Tools can include things like communication tools like sign language can we read sign language in space if suspended in weightless in zero-gravity. We can also learn a lot about how people with different types of bodies and different types of conditions function in a weightless environment. With this, we can learn how learn how to design the environments to better enable them to function, but also what strengths they may offer in doing so."

When listening into a podcast with one of your colleagues Dr. Sherri Wells Jensen, she discussed the concept of how there may be comparative advantages that folks with disability may have over able-bodied astronauts which can be learned and harnessed. That being said, what amount of your work, if any at all, is investigating potential parameters that may introduce strengths among those with disabilities in space flight?

"Good question, some of the lines of research are certainly around communication.

Thinking about the strengths question there, I think there's a number of things – individuals who are deaf, for example, there's the potential for avoiding motion sickness. There's also the fact that they already communicate nonverbally. So, if you're trying to communicate with another person in a space suit and modes of communication are out, they already have sort of an intuition for doing that.

Another example is considering how one could use a prosthetic in space? A prosthetic leg for example, may be replaced something that's useful, like a tool or a container where you can hold tools or something like that?

In that kind of environment, it's just a matter of figuring out what those strengths are in space, right, also considering how it may vary for each different sort of individual or type of disability perhaps. We're definitely still exploring those. And I'm sure that there's lots more to sort of find, but those are a few examples."

As we progress with MAA, you have so far successfully completed one parabolic flight with the next flight currently being organized and future flights in active discussion. That being said, what are your personal predictions regarding a long-term future outlook of what's being done? What types of impact expecting from this work?

"I mean the work we're doing is definitely making some waves in the industry. Obviously, the private space industry is growing incredibly quickly. Everything I do with my personal/professional work is public - NASA funded academic research, right?

However, when it comes to the private space industry, there's tons of space companies that are trying to build rockets to send people into space, and they have noticed the project. In no small part due to the fact that one of the directors, that is George Whitesides, who is very heavily involved in industry and has been able to make those connections for the project.

In terms of our goal, we already know that it's possible anybody could go to space and operate/function safely in space if and when we learn the right things. That being said, there's a lot of things we have to learn about what those people need.

We're not going to learn everything all at once, but our immediate goal is to learn things that can very urgently influence the way that these spacecrafts are being designed right now, because everybody's building them right now, right!

They're designing a new space station, they're building a new space shuttle, they're doing whatever. For those reasons, we want to get outcomes that can go into feed into what they are doing right now."

… in reference to the last question – so in a way, affecting design in real time?

"Exactly !

We (referring to scientists) should have started this work 30 years ago and had lots of time to do the research.

But we didn't.

Now we're here (referring to MAA) and everybody's building rockets, and we're just sort of doing what we can to give them as much information as they can to design those things excessively and hopefully encourage them to do so.

Not everybody is going to care. But I think that some of them do. Even public partners like ESA(European Space Agency) and NASA are starting to notice. I would expect that we'll see quite a bit of change on this over the next 5-10 years."

In essence, with everything that was discussed from your motivations to participating in MAA, to delving into what this project is investigation and the potential of long-term impacts that

can come as result – it seems that you and the entire MAA team is really at the cusp of something extraordinary for those with disabilities but also for the current understanding of space travel, space travel and who can take part within it. Considering how monumental this project may to humanity, do you have parting thoughts you'd would like share?

"Thinking about the moment in history were in - this isn't something with day-to-day conversation on the project and so I don't even necessarily know that I've really talked to most people about it – I think that it is an important moment in history right now.

There's a big question of who's controlling the narrative of what this moment is and what it means. In academic science there is a big tension, at least in my field, in, in planetary science. There's a big tension between excitement about activities that are happening in this area and apprehension about what it means.

Because the reality is, not everybody thinks that we should be going to space and I actually tend to fall more on that side, which sounds hilarious coming from the fact that I'm on this project right?

But, I am kind of a conservationist in that I don't think we should go settle on other worlds. I don't want to the surface of the moon or an asteroid by mining it. I'd rather study it. I want it to be beautiful. I want it to, to be nature.

In that context, I generally advocate for sending like less humans to space rather than more humans to space. But the fact is, I don't have control over whether or not private companies are going to do that. And that's ultimately why I still find this project really important because, if we are going to go to space at all, if we humans are going to go to space at all then it is important that everybody is included. Because those that actually go to space, will be helping to define why it is we're going there and what we're going to do when we get there. For example, if the only people sending people into space are people who want to mine. Then that's all that we're going to do and that's going to be the focus. Similarly, if the people going into space want to settle another world, that's what we're going to do.

I just think that it's really important that everybody's perspective as a society, it's important that that we include everybody's perspective in defining why should we explore space and what does exploration mean and what is our relationship to space going to be going forward as a civilization.

I think people ought to be aware of the concept that going into space isn't something that we as humans have to do. It's something that we're choosing to do and it's important that all of us are involved in what that means for us, right?

It shouldn't just be that, like, a couple of billionaires get to decide what our relationship to space should be. It should be something that all of us side, and therefore it is important that all perspectives are included in. In doing that with the upcoming moon activities will have the first woman and the first black woman on the moon, which is fantastic, and it's really important to get that perspective from all aspects of our society about what we're doing there.

With that I would like people to sort of think about. Why is it we're actually going to space? And who is going and it's t*he who* is going that this project of course is focused on.

And I'm sure that opinions on that vary within the team. But for me, that's what I see as the sort of the high-level importance of the work is defining that relationship between humanity and space and including more voices in developing that narrative."

Concluding Statement

Dr. Molaro's interview provided much more then plain insight as to what MAA is attempting to investigating with their space flight endeavours including people with disabilities. It provides and establishes an empirical case as to why the investigation of people with disabilities is much larger than attempt to inspire inclusivity, but rather it is an active attempt to employ a scientific lens towards analyzing and challenging what we currently understand about those who participate in space travel/space flight and how it can be enhanced. Simultaneously, MAA's work is occurring during a time of great innovation (as Dr.Molaro mentioned) and the insights developed from upcoming missions can be paramount in modifying current design to modify, accommodate and overall exemplify the experiences of those that can take part in space flight. Additionally, MAA's work not only actively forges an opportunity for everyone to be included in the relationship between humanity and the cosmos, but it also directly plays a role adhering to what humanity really is – everyone, rather then a select few.

References

Mission Astro Access. (2022, March 1). *About*. AstroAccess. https://astroaccess.org/about/

Planetary Science Institute. (2022, May 29). *PSI's Jamie Molaro discusses AstroAccess space program.* https://www.psi.edu/news/lpsc2022molaro

Chapter 8: Space Gondolas - How are They More Accessible to Disabled People than Rockets?

Margaret Choi

Humans have always longed to explore and unravel more mysteries about space, our constantly expanding universe that is seemingly void of matter and yet extremely fascinating (*"What is Space? - A Definition of Our Universe and Beyond | Space,"* n.d.). Speaking of space exploration, it is likely what first comes to most people's minds is a rocket, a vehicle with a jet engine powerful enough to carry people or equipment beyond Earth and out into space (*"How do space rockets work? - Explain that Stuff,"* n.d.). Rocketry was first tested more than 2,000 years ago (*"The History of Rockets | Space,"* n.d.). As early as 400 B.C., a Greek mathematician named Archytas experimented with a pseudo-rocket made of a wooden pigeon suspended on wires and propelled by escaping steam; 300 years later, the Greek mathematician Hero of Alexandria invented the aeolipile, a sphere-shaped device that could rotate with the help of steaming water (*"The History of Rockets | Space,"* n.d.). Over the centuries, with persistent hard work motivated by curiosity, humans finally made a huge milestone in the history of space exploration by launching the very first rocket — Sputnik — into space on October 4, 1957 (*"The History of Rockets | Space,"* n.d.). Just a couple of years following the success with Sputnik, the Soviet cosmonaut, Yuri Gagarin made a 108-minute orbital flight on April 12,

1961 (*"The History of Rockets | Space,"* n.d.). Since then, humans have made a number of advances in space exploration, and nowadays, rockets are routinely sent to space for satellites placement or cargo delivery (*"The History of Rockets | Space,"* n.d.). Progress has also been made throughout the past decades to include women and people of different ethnicity as the society becomes increasingly aware of the importance of diversity (*"NASA, ESA experts weigh in on diversity and inclusion in space,"*, n.d.). However, space-exploration is still far from being inclusive — there have been no physically disabled astronauts in space (*"NASA, ESA experts weigh in on diversity and inclusion in space,"*, n.d.). It is not only unfair to not include physically disabled astronauts, by not providing them the same chances, the field is missing out on fantastic talents and possibilities for further advancements too. Space exploration does not only depend on rockets. As technologies advance, maybe it is time to consider other means of travelling to provide greater accessibility and enable physically disabled people to delve into the wonders of space as well. One alternative means to travel to at least the higher layers of atmosphere is by stratospheric balloons, which are high-altitude balloons that get released into the stratosphere (the second layer of the atmosphere) (*"About stratospheric balloons | Canadian Space Agency,"*, n.d.). These balloons can be equipped with gondolas suspended on the flight chain, and the gondolas can hold up to 1.1 tons of weight (*"About stratospheric balloons | Canadian Space Agency,"*, n.d.). Typically, these gondolas are used for purposes such as weather forecasting and transporting equipment or crafts (*"About stratospheric balloons | Canadian Space Agency,"*, n.d.). In recent years, some companies have looked into the use of these space gondolas to give people a peak of Earth from a different perspective. In this article, we will look at how these space gondolas could be a more accessible option than rockets for people with physical disabilities who are enthusiastic about exploration.

One big advantage of the stratospheric balloons, or space gondolas, is their much lower costs than rockets, which makes them more accessible for not just people with physical disabilities, but everyone else as well. Stratospheric balloons are usually made of ultra-thin plastic, and once filled with helium, the plastic would swell and stretch into a gigantic tear-shaped balloon that can be as long as the height of the Eiffel Tower (*"Commercial balloons in the stratosphere could monitor hurricanes and scan for solar storms \ Science | AAAS,"*, n.d.; *"About stratospheric balloons | Canadian Space Agency,"*, n.d.). These balloons do not require engines or fuel, but can still conduct long-duration flights lasting for weeks or even months (*"About stratospheric balloons | Canadian Space Agency,"*, n.d.). World View Enterprises, an Arizona-based space tourism company, has developed such space gondolas that are expected to start carrying passengers in commercial flights lasting for five days at an altitude of at least 100,000 feet as early as year 2024 (*"World View to start flying passengers on stratospheric balloon rides in 2024 | Space,"*, n.d.). They expect that each seat in this space gondola would cost $50,000, which is significantly less than what other companies typically charge for commercial flights into space (*"World View to start flying passengers on stratospheric balloon rides in 2024 | Space,"*, n.d.). For instance, another company called Space Perspective sells trips to space as well, but instead of space gondolas, they employ rocket-powered crafts, and the price of just one ticket is $450,000 (*"World View to start flying passengers on stratospheric balloon rides in 2024 | Space,"*, n.d.). With the more affordable costs, it would be much more possible to accommodate more people using space gondolas as opposed to rockets. As physical disabilities such as deafness may require the company of interpreters, the better costs could possibly enable much more accommodations such as having interpreters or personal attendants go on board along with the disabled people, which is a huge benefit of using space gondolas. Additional retrofitting equipments can also cost more money, but as space gondolas cost much less than rocket flights, such equipments shall be included in the gondolas more easily than in rockets (*"A Future for People With Disabilities in Outer Space Takes Flight - The New York Times,"*, n.d.).

Space travel comes with potential health risks, with some being particularly concerning to people with certain disabilities. For example, when one experiences weightlessness for a prolonged period of time, the individual's bones can lose density (*"Preventing Bone Loss in Space Flight | NASA,"*, n.d.). This is because in a microgravity environment, there is reduced loading stimuli, which can lead to increased bone resorption while there is no change or decrease in bone formation, resulting in bone density loss at a rate as high as ten times that of osteoporosis (*"Preventing Bone Loss in Space Flight | NASA,"*, n.d.). For people with amputations, this loss in bone mass could negatively impact their balance (*"Can Technology Open Spaceflight to Disabled Astronauts? | WIRED,"* n.d.). This challenge can be tackled with space gondolas. According to World View Enterprise, the space gondolas can use pressurized seats, meaning that passengers could still walk around freely as if they were on the ground, reducing the health risks associated with weightlessness (*"Space Tourism and Exploration FAQs | About Stratospheric Space Tourism,"*, n.d.). In addition, weightlessness can lead to to skin rashes or irritations at where a prosthetic device meets the residual limb due to a number of reasons such as disruption of the skin surface microbiota, and having infections at such sites could cause discomfort throughout the trip (Farkas & Farkas, 2021; *"Can Technology Open Spaceflight to Disabled Astronauts? | WIRED,"* n.d.). With space gondolas offering pressurized seats, there would be a much lower risk for such health problems. Passengers on space gondolas can also wear normal clothing thanks to these seats, unlike on rockets, where spacesuits are required, and this could also likely provide more comfort and individuals with prosthetics move around with greater ease (*"Space Tourism and Exploration FAQs | About Stratospheric Space Tourism,"*, n.d.). The design of space suits that can fit people using prosthetics would take time, but if normal clothing is allowed, then the goal of getting closer to space can be fulfilled sooner with space gondolas!

As mentioned above, since the gondolas have pressurized seats, passengers on board may not experience weightlessness, and this could be a letdown. Nonetheless, space gondolas are still an excellent alternative to rockets for those looking to see the spectacular view of Earth from high altitudes. On the brightside, without weightlessness, passengers would not require as much training. To prepare for weightlessness, it takes lots of intensive training. For example, NASA would put its astronauts on parabolic flights to simulate the condition of being in a weightless space (*"How astronauts prepare for weightlessness explained | Britannica,"* n.d.). To reduce risks for bone density loss, they would also need to rigorously exercise their bodies both beforehand and during their time in space (*"NASA - Your Body in Space: Use it or Lose it,"* n.d.). The time saved from not needing to go through such rigorous training could be used to conduct research and strengthen other technical skill sets, equipping one with more knowledge about space.

Another advantage that could make space gondolas an appealing alternative for getting off Earth's surface is its safety, which is relevant to every single one of us. Unlike rockets, the stratospheric balloons are filled with helium, a safe and non-flammable gas that wouldn't poes the risk of explosions as in the case of rockets, which are fueled by combustion using liquid oxygen and hydrogen (*"Rocket fuel - Rocketology: NASA's Space Launch System,"* n.d.). Balloon physics are also predictable, allowing for better accuracy or precision in the prediction of landing in cases of emergency (*"Space Tourism and Exploration FAQs | About Stratospheric Space Tourism,"*, n.d.). Moreover, the balloons can be recycled after the flights, which can help reduce waste and make these flights even more sustainable than rockets which emit large amounts of carbon dioxide and pollutants harmful to the environment every time it launches (*"The Coming Surge of Rocket Emissions - Eos,"* n.d.).

Nevertheless, it is important to note that while these space gondolas are seemingly able to bring one to extreme heights and present to its passengers the fascinating views, there are limitations. These space gondolas are dependent on the use of stratospheric balloons. The stratospheric balloons, as their name implies, can only reach the stratosphere, which is about 15 to 45 km in altitude (*"About stratospheric balloons | Canadian Space Agency,"*, n.d.). It refers to the atmosphere layer above troposphere, in which parabolic flights and commercial flights take place (*"About stratospheric balloons | Canadian Space Agency,"*, n.d.). On the other hand, rockets can travel to an altitude as high as 950 km before falling back to Earth (*"Getting rockets into space — Science Learning Hub,"*, n.d.). This means, even though these space gondolas may be more accessible to the disabled in many different ways and offer great benefits such as smaller amounts of and more environmentally friendly fuels, they are not meant to replace rockets, and there are still a large number of things which these gondolas are unable to achieve. However, for the sole purpose of exploring the realms high above the Earth's surface and setting foot into the field of space exploration, space gondolas remain to be a great option. We have witnessed how fast our technologies improve, and perhaps in the near future, there would be a much more advanced way to send these gondolas to altitudes beyond our imagination right now.

Space is full of wonders and should be for everyone. Our society is becoming more and more aware of how important it is to be inclusive. Step by step, we are tackling this caveat in our system and improving gradually. There used to be no women or people of colour being astronauts, but thankfully this has changed. To be truly inclusive, we should take people from all backgrounds and of different body types into consideration, and by backgrounds, it does not necessarily refer to just the ethnicity backgrounds. It would be an understatement to say that our present system has already evolved enough just because there are now astronauts of varying genders, ethnicity, and skin colours. One group of people that society seems to overlook is those who are disabled. There have been no disabled astronauts in history. It may be easy for the challenges that come along with having physically disabled astronauts to overshadow how some skills they have naturally developed could be beneficial to working in space. For instance, hearing-impaired astronauts who are fluent in American Sign Language (ASL) would not be bothered by the loud noises that result from the operation of the machines and could still communicate with others in space in case there are technical difficulties with the radio. Recently, the European Space Agency (ESA) is looking to change this by helping disabled individuals become astronauts too (*"ESA - Parastronaut feasibility project,"* n.d.). As this has never been done before, there needs to be modifications to a number of things such as safety protocols, space suits, accommodations on the crafts, specialized training etc. Such technological advances may require some more time to make the dreams of disabled astronauts come true. Nevertheless, there are also other ways to get closer to space as various companies begin to offer commercial flights through rocket-powered crafts. These flights are, however, very costly and just the cost alone could greatly reduce its accessibility for not only disabled people, but also for the majority of the general population. Space gondolas rely on stratospheric balloons and offer a more accessible and affordable alternative for disabled people. These gondolas cost significantly less than rockets, which could in turn help preserve funding to be used for better equipment that can increase accessibility and comfort for disabled passengers. In addition, these space gondolas can help resolve some concerns. As these gondolas can include pressurized seats, health risks associated with prolonged presence in weightlessness such as bone mass loss can be lowered. These space gondolas are fueled using helium in the balloons and do not emit pollutants like the rockets do. The balloons can also be recycled after each flight, making them not only have better accessibility, but also much more environmentally friendly. While these gondolas may not provide the same experience as rockets, they are for sure a great start for anyone who wants to embark on a journey to explore space, as the view they provide is no less beautiful than that given by rocket rides. If these space gondolas could succeed in carrying both people with or without disabilities to that far above Earth, it could spark someone's interest and passion about becoming an astronaut, or serve as a stepping stone for longer trips in the future. With the continued effort and advances in technologies, it is hopeful that one day these space gondolas can reach the further parts of space while accommodating more people with different bodies, giving more people the chance to pursue their dreams and make them a reality.

References

A Future for People With Disabilities in Outer Space Takes Flight - The New York Times. (n.d.). Retrieved August 16, 2022, from https://www.nytimes.com/2021/10/22/science/astronauts-disabilities-astroaccess.html
About stratospheric balloons | Canadian Space Agency. (n.d.). Retrieved August 16, 2022, from https://www.asc-csa.gc.ca/eng/sciences/balloons/about-stratospheric-balloons.asp
Can Technology Open Spaceflight to Disabled Astronauts? | WIRED. (n.d.). Retrieved August 16, 2022, from https://www.wired.com/story/can-technology-open-spaceflight-to-disabled-astronauts/
Commercial balloons in the stratosphere could monitor hurricanes and scan for solar storms | Science | AAAS. (n.d.). Retrieved August 16, 2022, from https://www.science.org/content/article/commercial-balloons-stratosphere-could-monitor-hurricanes-and-scan-solar-storms
ESA - Parastronaut feasibility project. (n.d.). Retrieved August 16,

2022, from https://www.esa.int/About_Us/Careers_at_ESA/ESA_Astronaut_Selection/Parastronaut_feasibility_project

Farkas, Á., & Farkas, G. (2021). Effects of Spaceflight on Human Skin. *Skin Pharmacology and Physiology, 34*(5), 239–245. https://doi.org/10.1159/000515963

Getting rockets into space — Science Learning Hub. (n.d.). Retrieved August 24, 2022, from https://www.sciencelearn.org.nz/resources/394-getting-rockets-into-space

How astronauts prepare for weightlessness explained | Britannica. (n.d.). Retrieved August 16, 2022, from https://www.britannica.com/video/153024/Description-weightlessness-astronauts

How do space rockets work? - Explain that Stuff. (n.d.). Retrieved August 16, 2022, from https://www.explainthatstuff.com/spacerockets.html

NASA - Your Body in Space: Use It or Lose It. (n.d.). Retrieved August 16, 2022, from https://www.nasa.gov/audience/forstudents/5-8/features/F_Your_Body_in_Space.html

NASA - Yuri Gagarin: First Man in Space. (n.d.). Retrieved August 16, 2022, from https://www.nasa.gov/mission_pages/shuttle/sts1/gagarin_anniversary.html

NASA, ESA experts weigh in on diversity and inclusion in space | Space. (n.d.). Retrieved August 16, 2022, from https://www.space.com/spaceflight-diversity-nasa-esa

Preventing Bone Loss in Space Flight | NASA. (n.d.). Retrieved August 16, 2022, from https://www.nasa.gov/mission_pages/station/research/benefits/bone_loss.html

rocket fuel – Rocketology: NASA's Space Launch System. (n.d.). Retrieved August 16, 2022, from https://blogs.nasa.gov/Rocketology/tag/rocket-fuel/

Space Tourism and Exploration FAQs | About Stratospheric Space Tourism. (n.d.). Retrieved August 16, 2022, from https://worldview.space/technology-and-safety/

The Coming Surge of Rocket Emissions - Eos. (n.d.). Retrieved August 16, 2022, from https://eos.org/features/the-coming-surge-of-rocket-emissions

The History of Rockets | Space. (n.d.). Retrieved August 16, 2022, from https://www.space.com/29295-rocket-history.html

What Is Space? - A Definition of Our Universe and Beyond | Space. (n.d.). Retrieved August 16, 2022, from https://www.space.com/24870-what-is-space.html

World View to start flying passengers on stratospheric balloon rides in 2024 | Space. (n.d.). Retrieved August 16, 2022, from https://www.space.com/world-view-space-tourism-stratosphere-balloon

Chapter 9: Criteria for an Astronaut, Justin Baldi

Chitrini Tandon

For many years people have had very specific criteria for what an astronaut should look like. They will often consider someone who is extremely fit, extremely intelligent, and fits the idea of a "perfect" human which we have created as being an ideal candidate for an astronaut. But, what if that doesn't necessarily have to be true? What if there is more than one way of looking at it, and what if I told you we have the capabilities of implementing changes to make space exploration more accessible? Mission Astro: Access is a project dedicated to making space exploration more accessible to individuals who are disabled (2022). Together with Zero Gravity Corporation, they are working to send disabled scientists, veterans, students, athletes, and artists on parabolic flights (2022). Through this experience, the "AstroAccess Ambassadors" will experience lunar gravity, Martian gravity, and zero gravity while conducting various experiments and gathering observations (2022). Lunar gravity is the gravitational pull of the Moon's surface, it is about one-sixth (about 16%) of Earth's gravity and is 1.62 m/s² (2022). Martian gravity is 3.721 m/s² and is a little more than one-third of Earth's gravity (about 38%) ("Ask an astronomer"). And zero gravity is when gravity is 0 m/s² and a state of weightlessness is experienced ("What is zero gravity?"). For reference, the gravity on Earth is 9.807 m/s².

One member of this team is Justin Baldi who is an ASL interpreter. Justin is a child of a deaf adult (CODA) and has been interpreting his entire life. He has been professionally interpreting since 2001 and has specialized in Science, Technical, Educational, and Government interpreting (Media). Baldi works at NASA and has been a part of Mission Astro: Access. While he has always been interpreting he didn't realize that he would be interested in interpreting professionally until university. He was originally interested in aerospace engineering due to his interest in science but found his passion for professionally interpreting in college. During an interview with Justin he mentioned, "I liked it a lot more than I thought because growing up I did not want to be an interpreter." After working as an interpreter for a few years he was recruited into NASA, he said "someone who was working at NASA as an interpreter saw me and said he would be a good fit, not realizing my background, [I] started joining and then [they found] out that my background really did make me a good fit." While at NASA, Justin worked with the technical department, with engineers, and on projects related to spacecrafts, computer science, and others. And through his work at NASA he was asked to be a part of Mission Astro: Access. One of Justin's consumers became an ambassador for Mission Astro: Access which was his first introduction to the program. While he initially assisted through being the interpreter for an interview with his consumer they asked him to be part of flight one. When offered the position Justin thought, "sure, why not, this is a great experience, [I] didn't know fully what to expect." Both Justin and his consumer were accepted into the program. He will continue to work on this project on continuing flights and as the interpret coordinator for Mission Astro: Access.

In Justin's words Mission Astro: Access is an important project because "every disadvantaged community needs an advocate, and I think that this is a great avenue to advocate in the next frontier which is space." Space is considered to be the next frontier and advocating for the disabled community in space travel is important. The earlier we start the better. According to Baldi, it is easier to design accessibility from the beginning rather than trying to implement changes after systems have been put in place or attempting to modify them, "doing it on the ground floor, doing it at the beginning is much more helpful than doing it at the end." For example, if space stations are currently being designed it is important to get feedback on what will help the disabled community now. This project is just one facet of increasing accessibility and equity. The physical experiments are one benefit of Mission Astro: Access, it allows scientists to prove that it is possible to send disabled folks into space with some accommodations. But, Justin believes that through Mission Astro: Access they have the opportunity to be role models for others at the same time as doing experiments to increase accessibility. The ambassadors specifically have the opportunity to be role models for individuals with various disabilities. In Baldi's words, this project helps to create a mindset of "you have done this already so I can do it as well, or some portion of it." This project allows them to create a family and gives individuals the opportunity to feel connected and have someone to talk to, it creates the opportunity for individuals with disabilities to reach out to those with disabilities in higher positions and provides them with support to help reach their goals and feel a connection to others. Mission Astro: Access provides a crucial resource that has not been available before.

While working with Mission Astro: Access Justin has had the opportunity to be a part of two flights. Flight one had four overarching goals, the one related to Justin's position was "Communication Accessibility". This included answering two questions; 1) "How is American Sign Language legibility impacted by floating in microgravity?" and 2) "How will important safety cues, traditionally only shared verbally, be efficiently communicated to Deaf and hard of hearing crew members?" (2022). The other goals were "Physical Environment Accessibility", "Safety Procedures", and "General

Microgravity Research". During the first flight, as an interpreter, Justin took a back seat and let the other two deaf ambassadors experience as much as possible. During this flight, the deaf ambassadors were allowed to experience the flight and do their own work. There were experiments done related to the lighting system and ASL communication. While there was an attempt to do ASL communication it wasn't successful due to running out of time and it being their first time on the flight. On a second flight, Baldi had a bigger role and ASL communication was attempted in various different orientations such as inverted and transverse. The ASL communication was attempted between Baldi and one of his consumers. Currently, details of the experiment cannot be given but overall they found that they could understand each other more than they had originally thought as long as they could keep each other positioned in their field of vision. In the future, they will continue to understand ASL communication during flight and utilize a bigger sample size with more representation such as individuals who are late learners of ASL, completely deaf, hard of hearing, early learners of sign language, etc to diversify the sample. Future research will also focus on different variations of ASL grammar and different orientations.

When asked about the best experience he has had with Mission Astro: Access, Baldi describes the family that he has found during flight one to be the most rewarding part of the program. When first asked to take part in the flight, his initial thoughts were "Holy crap, I'm going on a zero-G flight…I never in my wildest dreams thought I would do that." He explains how on the entire journey to Long Beach, the location of flight one, his excitement built up, getting to experience parabolic flight is not something someone gets to do every day. But, as he got closer and closer to actually taking off, he became less excited about the flight itself and more about the people he was surrounded by. This group of individuals had only met once virtually but when they got there they felt like family, "It felt like a family very quickly. There were very quickly inside jokes going around, very quickly [there were] people working with each other, and it was very fun. It was very fun to see… and be a part of," he continued on to say, "Even though I wasn't fully in it with the group of ambassadors, I was kind of on the fringe, it was just so fascinating to see how this group of people were able to come together and become one." Baldi describes this as a fun experience to be a part of and one that he will keep with him for a long time.

The Astro Access website states that "Outer space is not just humanity's future: It's a call to rethink life on Earth today," (2022). For Justin, this means understanding where we are now and how we can move forward and change lives. Any big revolution, as many have happened throughout history, such as the internet or electricity, should allow people to change their lives and it is important to gain an understanding of how it will change lives, we need to think "how is this going to change lives, where are we now and how can this help improve it. And with that being said, going to space, [the question is] how can going to space help improve life on earth." According to Baldi, it is important to explore new worlds, and new science, and give people here on Earth a new life. It is important to take the opportunity we have been given in the correct way and use our gifts for good. Furthermore, Justin believes that it is important to realize that inclusion is not scary and it isn't hard either. He adds, "A lot of people don't go near this topic for one of two reasons, either it's going to cost them money, or they don't know what to do and are scared to do something wrong, so they just don't do anything at all. I think that if they were to take the time to talk to someone that was physically disabled or needed special accommodations or whatever the case may be, they'll realize that they are just a person and you can just talk to them usually… the bulk of the people are willing to work with everybody [and] are willing to work with someone trying to give them accommodations." When we realize that we are all just human beings and we take the time to talk to each other and to get to know one another we realize that it is a lot simpler to make changes towards equity and inclusion than we originally might have thought of. Often, people might fear the cost of change or the fear of "doing something wrong" and making a mistake might deter people from even looking into change but it can be done and done so smoothly.

When considering the future of space exploration, Baldi "wishes [he] could see the future as this bright idea of a utopia where everyone is in harmony and agrees with each other. But, I don't see that unfortunately, that is just not what humans are." He would thou like to see a better understanding and acceptance of people who are different, regardless of it being race, disability, sexuality, or anything else. He hopes for a future where we can all understand each other better and work together. From his point of view, even if we moved to another planet there most likely won't be a "utopia", "it would be just like moving to another continent… we would just create another society that still has problems."

Mission Astro: Access has been an experience Justin Baldi will never forget. Justin is one of many members of the Mission Astro: Access team and has had the opportunity to participate in two flights. About 15% of the world identifies as disabled, this mission will not only improve accessibility to space exploration but will have a bigger impact on improving the lives of individuals living on Earth with disability (2022). Justin hopes to continue to aid in creating a better future where there is increased inclusion and accessibility. Mission Astro: Access is currently preparing for their second flight which is currently planned to take place on November 19, 2022, in Fort Lauderdale, Florida.

References

Ask an astronomer. Cool Cosmos. (n.d.). Retrieved September 3, 2022, from https://coolcosmos.ipac.caltech.edu/ask/73-How-strong-is-the-gravity-on-Mars-

Disability inclusion overview. World Bank. (2022). Retrieved September 3, 2022, from https://www.worldbank.org/en/topic/

disability#:~:text=Results-,One%20billion%20people%2C%20or%20 15%25%20of%20the%20world%27s%20population%2C,is%20 higher%20for%20developing%20countries.

Lunar gravity. Oxford Reference. (2022). Retrieved September 3, 2022, from https://www.oxfordreference.com/view/10.1093/oi/authority.20110803100118823

Media, L. C. (n.d.). *Independent interpreters*. Independent Interpreters | Interpreter Profile for Justin Baldi - Washington, D.C., Virginia and Maryland / Independent freelance direct hire local ASL sign language interpreters. Retrieved September 3, 2022, from https://independentinterpreters.com/profile/Justin-Baldi

Mission Astro: Access. AstroAccess. (2022, March 1). Retrieved September 3, 2022, from https://astroaccess.org/about/

What is zero gravity? definition of zero gravity, zero gravity meaning. The Economic Times. (n.d.). Retrieved September 3, 2022, from https://economictimes.indiatimes.com/definition/zero-gravity

Chapter 10: Planning and Risk, Dr. Sheri Wells-Jensen

By Ying Yi Feng

NASA has been researching the dangers and risks of the space environment since its inception in 1958. Since the 1960s, the federal government and the space industry have been engaged in the commercialization of space. With the launch of the International Space Station (ISS) in 1969, the potential for commercialization of space expanded. Since then, as space exploration activities have escalated, and space research and technology has grown tremendously (Marge, 2022). Despite space being a dangerous place, it piques the imagination and interest of millions of people. However, most will learn that they do not meet, and will never fulfill, the job's non-negotiable physical criteria. They are either overly tall or have a weak knee, flat feet, or some minor but uncorrectable physiological anomaly (Wells-Jensen, 2018). According to the current conventional regulations and space craft and space equipment design, they are not designed to accommodate astronauts with disabilities. There is no easy method to change out handicapped personnel in space, and due to limited resources and cramped living circumstances, they cannot afford to feed, protect, and provide air for those who are not contributing (Wells-Jensen, n.d.).
A blind person aboard a space station may appear alarming at first glance, considering that their colleagues may have to rely on them in an emergency. However, these individuals are successful parents, teachers,

scientists, and chefs, and do not have more accidents than sighted people (Wells-Jensen, 2018). These rigid rules deter so many people from becoming astronauts, such as people with disabilities, despite the potential advantages they may offer for space travel.

Dr. Sheri Wells-Jensen is a linguistic professor at Bowling Green State University in Ohio. Her teaching and research interests include applied phonology and syntax, astrobiology, braille, disability studies, language creation, language preservation, psycholinguistics, speech production, and xenolinguistics. She is one of the Project Leads and Ambassadors for the Mission: Astro Access Project and one of the individuals who flew on Flight 1. After presenting her article from the Scientific American titled, "The Case for Disabled Astronauts" at a conference, she was asked by the CEO of Mission: Astro Access, Anna Voelker, if she would be interested in joining the project. They were both interested in working with increasing the number of disabled students in the STEM field. As Dr. Wells-Jensen was present during the initial stages of the project and being blind herself, she helped objectively select the non-blind crew for Flight 1. Sifting through the large volumes of high calibre applicants, she and the rest of the team were able to narrow it down to 12 individuals. The project aimed to address issues of accessibility in space travel and since a holistic view was needed, individuals with varying physical and sensory disabilities were selected. The individuals chosen to board Flight 1 stood out because of their strong passion and belief in the project as they understood why increasing accessibility needed to start with space travel. This is important as Dr. Wells-Jensen states that "This is the right time to do it because we're just starting out".

With the flight science foundation and in partnership with other contributors and sponsors, the Mission: Astro Access team were able to charter the Zero G plane to make this dream a reality. The Zero G plane is modified such that the seats in the front two thirds of the plane were taken out and replaced with mats that lined all four walls of the plane. As the plane makes parabolic flights, individuals are able to experience a weightless environment. Dr. Wells-Jensen recounts lying on her back while the plane took a hard angle upward before tipping forward and thinking to herself, "Oh, this can be terrifying", as she felt the nose of the plane going down. However, instead of feeling like they were plunging towards the earth, she felt gravity going away and the sensation of falling disappeared. She remembered thinking, "That's weird. There's air between me and the ground. I didn't feel myself lifting up. It was amazing."

While in the air, the crew members had research experiments to test out to see what can and cannot be done to determine the types of changes that need to be made to ensure that the flight is more accessible. This included modifications to the space vessel as well as to their spacesuits. Dr. Wells-Jensen was tasked with performing a few experiments that saw both success and failure. For the orientation, the team tried to use sound beacons, which are navigation devices that emit periodic sounds so that blind and visually impaired individuals can locate objects in their surroundings, but they found that the plane was too loud. While using the sound beacon was ineffective on the plane, Dr. Wells-Jensen was able to successfully write with a slate and stylus, which are one of the ways to write braille. Additionally, she was tasked with using a haptic device to determine its effectiveness in communicating commands.

The results and impact of having successfully completed flight 1 is pivotal and imperative in changing the narrative of conventional space travel. The rigorous demand for astronauts to have the near-perfect physiological state greatly eliminates otherwise qualified contenders, namely individuals with disabilities. This standard is impractical as astronauts will all experience a loss of bone mass and be exposed to heightened levels of radiation during long space flights (Wells-Jensen,

2018) that will ultimately impair their ability to function at their original, maximal level. Rather than having to make many adjustments, having a diverse crew such as a blind astronaut is the sensible and wise thing to do. Not only will blind astronauts not experience nausea from the lack of a visual horizon or be disorientated by the intimidating view of space walks, but they will also not be affected by the harm done to their vision by microgravity, that causes fluid to collect in the eye, distorting the eyeball, or pushing on the optic nerve (Wells-Jensen, 2018). As one spends more time in space on missions, the more likely it is that accidents such as injury or disease can occur that may impair one's body and senses. It can be quite difficult cognitively and emotionally to adjust from being an active, confident, able-bodied person to becoming an active, confident person with a disability. However, this transition can be less complicated and more straightforward if the adaptive equipment is already implemented and if there are active and confident disabled crew members available to assist (Wells-Jensen, 2018). The idea is that whatever disability the astronauts may encounter, they will have the proper environment set up so that they may continue their space journey as safely and efficiently as possible.

Without taking proactive measures to design space crafts and space suits that are adaptable and accommodating, space flight can become quite dangerous as astronauts become restricted by their limiting environment and are left to navigate their surroundings without proper guidance. Spacecrafts are designed to maximize safety by having extra oxygen tanks, backup computers, and etc…, so if one component fails or gets broken, there is a spare component waiting to take its place. This logic can be applied to implementing accessible equipment that was adapted for a blind astronaut as it would act as an additional layer of defense against mission failure, and it could possibly aid sighted astronauts in the dark. A mixture of soap and tears in Canadian astronaut Chris Hadfield temporarily blinded him during his spacewalk in 2001. While one issue was that he could not see, the larger problem at hand was that the present spacesuit design forced astronauts to depend too much on hand-eye coordination at the expense of other vital sensory information. The objective for blind astronauts would be to build suits with more flexibility and tactile input, allowing the hands to be utilised more readily to explore and use instruments (Wells-Jensen, 2018). Proper procedures and accommodations should be a guarantee as it is their ethical responsibility to ensure that they are doing their utmost to keep the astronauts safe before, during and after their flight.

About 15% of the world, estimated to be around 1 billion people, identify as having a disability, making them the world's largest minority (United Nations, n.d.). From an economic standpoint, it would be ill-advised for the space industry to needlessly eliminate a significant portion of their customer base. It would also be financially advantageous to implement the design accommodations early on rather than remodelling later as this will incur higher costs and it may not even be feasible to do. From a practical standpoint, when products and environments follow the Principles of Universal design, it becomes safer and more convenient for everyone. Universal Design is "a design process that enables and empowers a diverse population by improving human performance, health and wellness, and social participation". An everyday example of this is curb cuts (University at Buffalo, 2022). They are not only practical for people with mobility issues but also other individuals that are pulling a backpack or suitcase, pushing a stroller or even those who are not paying attention and do not want to trip over a step. If an accident were to occur where the lights on the space craft goes out, a sighted astronaut will likely look for a light source like a flashlight to ensure visual access to the environment. Even if the emergency lights come on, it may take a while for their eyes to adjust. While this is occurring, a blind astronaut, unaffected by the changes in light levels, can head over to the source of the problem. In a more dire situation, such as the fire that occurred in 1997 on the Russian Mir space station, the astronauts struggled to locate one of the fire extinguishers as the smoke from the fire obscured their view. Even though the blind astronaut will be affected by the lack of good air, they will be able to navigate their surroundings and look for the fire extinguisher at the source of heat and noise despite the thick smoke. The requirements of a blind crew would entail stringent procedures to minimise disorganized clutter (Wells-Jensen, 2018).

By anticipating the situations that may arise as individuals begin to spend prolonged periods of time in space, space travel becomes safer and more efficient for everyone. This means that more research is needed to determine what still needs to be done to modify the current model space craft, space suits, and other space equipment. Dr. Wells-Jensen will also be boarding Flight 2, which is scheduled to occur later this year. "[There will be a] wider variety of scientific investigations and a wider variety of people", said Dr. Wells-Jensen about what to expect for Flight 2. Flight 2 will focus on expanding upon what was done on Flight 1 including performing experiments that they did not get to do on Flight 1 as well as new experiments to determine new and improved ways to modify space travel. "The joy of being in leadership positions in this group is that they're very dedicated, kind, and smart. People are very willing to work together to put the mission first."

Since the start of the commercialization of space, little has been done to make it more accessible for everyone as the current regulations for the near-perfect physiological state required to become an astronaut does more harm than good. In 2020, discussions of the prospect of civilians travelling, living and working in space in the coming future took at the White House National Space Council (Marge, 2022), which emphasizes the need for the inclusion of disabled astronauts in space. Dr. Wells-Jensen and the rest of the team at Mission: Astro Access have challenged this notion by flying on the Zero G plane and performing experiments to advance disability inclusion in space. "And doing this thing that has never been done before. 99.99% of humanity hasn't experienced zero gravity. It's kind of amazing", details Dr. Wells-Jensen. "It's our obligation then to use that experience for everyone's benefit and do what we can to communicate with people about why we did it and what disabled people can contribute to outer space exploration and how we can make things better for everybody". By determining what can and cannot be done during these flights, they are improving space travel as per the Principles of Universal Design, allowing everyone the opportunity to thrive in space.

References

The goals and benefits of Universal Design. Accessibility at UB - University at Buffalo. (2022,
January 14). Retrieved September 1, 2022, from https://www.buffalo.edu/access/help-and-support/topic3.html

Marge, M. (2022). Preparing individuals with disabilities for space travel and habitation.
Disability and Health Journal, 15(2), 101228. https://doi.org/10.1016/j.dhjo.2021.101228

United Nations. (n.d.). *Factsheet on persons with Disabilities Enable.* Retrieved September 1,
2022, from https://www.un.org/development/desa/disabilities/resources/factsheet-on-persons-with-disabilities.html

Wells-Jensen, S. (2018, May 30). *The case for disabled astronauts.* Scientific American Blog
Network. Retrieved August 25, 2022, from https://blogs.scientificamerican.com/observations/the-case-for-disabled-astronauts/

Wells-Jensen, S. (n.d.). *Dr. Sheri Wells-Jensen.* Retrieved September 2, 2022, from http://www.sheriwellsjensen.com/

Chapter 11 - Taking Off with Dana Bolles and Mission AstroAccess

Eddrick Lee

Meet Dana Bolles

Dana Bolles is an advocate who knows no limits to what she can do in life. She started her journey in Norwalk, California, where she grew up in a modest household with a supportive family. Education was always prioritized and manifested into Dana's life motto, "do not think about what you could do, just do it." After high school, Dana pursued a Bachelor of Science in Mechanical Engineering at California State University and graduated in 1993. During her master's certificate in Rehabilitation Engineering and Technology at San Francisco State University, she was offered a job in payload safety engineering by NASA. Since then, she has held many positions and currently works in science communications at NASA Headquarters. Dana contemplates that joining NASA was the best decision of her life, and she has been with the agency for 27 years. Also, Dana Bolles is a long-time advocate for people with disabilities. Dana sees having a disability as often having unique advantages, and she has been a part of programs that maximize the capacities people hold. For instance, she is an ambassador for the American Association for the Advancement of Science IF/THEN Initiative, which encourages young girls pursuing STEM careers. Fun fact: Dana's favourite space movie is The Martian, starring Matt Damon.

Star

Dana Bolles' experiences living outside the status quo led her to adopt a fulfilled, resilient, and non-judgemental identity. For one, Dana lends much of her success in life to her perception of competence. During my interview with Dana, she stressed the importance of making your own fate and not letting your disabilities derail you. Dana advised that we must understand our strengths and learn to play by them. Likewise, she impresses that the best indicator of success is not what your body can do but your perception of self. Dana is an engineer, science communications specialist, and ambassador for social justice. Also, Dana is one of the most resilient characters I have ever talked to. In the interview, she attributes her resilience to her sense of belonging to a bigger-picture organization, such as being an ambassador for Mission AstroAccess. She stipulates her adversities have made her define herself by her strengths rather than her vulnerabilities. Her positive outlook on experiences reminds me of other successful people who lived with disabilities in history. Lastly, when I asked Dana to describe her personality, she quickly responded by saying she is a non-judgemental person. Dana believes that being non-judgemental has allowed her to open her eyes to helping communities and individuals like herself. Dana associates her accepting attitude with the mindset of her disability. She does not blame others for her disability, so she never feels entitled. Consequently, Dana Bolles shines fiery and bright, like the stars in the sky.

Gravity

It does not get more inspiring than this story. Dana has conquered the societal expectations of a person living with a disability, a member of the LGBTQ community, and a woman of colour. Dana is proud of her unique intersecting identity, which helps her to feel a connection with various groups during her advocacy work. Dana is a fantastic source of inspiration and a positive role model for everyone.

Dana's specific contributions to the community consist of public outreach and using her voice to influence others. She has been featured on different platforms, from podcasts to blog sites, telling her life story and creating change. Dana is also an ambassador for girls in middle school who want to get into STEM. Dana uses words of support to empower young women and plans to end stigmas associated with female representation in the field. During our conversation, Dana remarked, "I try really hard when I do public speaking to help these communities and encourage people." Dana understands the importance of her advocacy work in combating public stigmas that carry negative attitudes towards women in STEM and individuals with disabilities. For example, Dana explained that she became a Mission AstroAccess Ambassador because she sought to reduce social barriers in opportunities for people with disabilities in space. Her advocacy work is moving and resonated with me deeply on a personal level.

Lift Off

Dana Bolles wants nothing more than getting astronauts with disabilities into space. She believes it would be a historical milestone and push the envelope of how we think of disabilities as a whole. During my interview, I chose to ask her, "what do you have to say to people with disabilities who want to go to space?" She replied, "I say, if you want to go to space, then do everything you can to get there." Did I forget to mention she is a very driven character? Dana also added that there are more opportunities than ever for people with disabilities to go to space. Backtrack a few decades ago, and the chances of a person with disabilities going into space were slim to none.

Thrusters

"Sometimes you have to reach out and rely on the people who love you most and want to help," said Dana Bolles while we spoke on confronting disabilities. Throughout our talk, Dana Bolles was emphatic about striving for family unity to overcome hardships in life. She argued that a strong sense of belonging allowed her to claim a positive identity of her disability which helped motivate her through those tough times. "You need to surround yourself with the support you need, whether it's services, people, your friends, or family, as long as they are positive," Dana added. Overall, she alleges that social support is related to self-confidence and a positive impression of self in people with disabilities.

While there is support, there are also haters. Dana Bolles proposes that people with disabilities have their fair share of naysayers. Dana exclaimed, "Like all obstacles, there will always be negative people who do not believe in you, such as growing up in an abusive family that tells you you are worth nothing." Dana's recommendation for people impacted by negative talk is to reach out for help and not to get stuck in the moment. "Remember that when you have times that are hard, and there are always going to be times that are hard, you can never let them stop you," Dana added. If we think about those moments too much, we become miserable. Sometimes, they happen for good reason because we can learn from those experiences.

Breaking Orbit

Dana Bolles expresses strong feelings about being misinterpreted because of her disabilities. She believes that people with disabilities can achieve just as much as those who do not have them, if not even more.

"You know, too often people look at us, and their initial thoughts about us are the things we can not do right," said Dana, "what they should be thinking is wow, I wonder all the cool things that you could do." I then asked Dana how we could minimize the stigmas of disabilities. Dana responded, "we need to start training people so when they see somebody with a disability, they do not just see them as some helpless little person but be curious about what they could do."

Dana's view on misinterpretation also stems from her personal experiences. She acknowledged that she was misjudged several times because of her status. Dana shared one specific encounter in the interview. Dana had arrived at Costco one day a little earlier before opening, and a security guard was trying to separate two flatbed trucks stuck together. Noticing the struggle, Dana offered to help the security guard, to which he responded with laughter. Dana is puzzled whenever people laugh when she offers to help. Dana then used her chair to open the lock connecting the trucks and went about her day. Dana cherishes this experience because it testifies people with disabilities can do extraordinary things.

Dana's view correlates with the message Mission AstroAccess is trying to convey by sending ambassadors with disabilities on Zero-G flights. "We could be great astronauts too if given the chance and mission," said Dana. The reality is that there is so much discrimination in our world towards people with disabilities and our assumptions of their limitations. Paving an example for disability inclusion in space travel not only benefits aspiring disabled astronauts but also gives hope for the future of humanity.

Detach

During our conversation, I became interested in how Mission

AstroAccess selects its ambassadors to go on Zero-G flights. Each flight had only 12 crew members, so there must have been a specific recruitment process to choose their lucky few. Dana was open to describing what she had to go through to become a Mission AstroAccess Ambassador. "Everything about the application process was done online," answered Dana, "you had to answer essay-style questions with word limits." "Once that is done, you will also have to submit a quick two-minute video on why you would want to join this mission," Dana further mentioned. This application was all held on the Mission AstroAccess site. A lot of work must go into the application process, and it does take a fair bit of time. However, if you get selected, the feeling and benefits of being an ambassador are priceless. Dana told me that getting accepted was one of the most thrilling moments of her life.

Space

Dana Bolles described that nothing on Earth amounts to feeling weightless on a Zero-G flight. "It feels incredible," Dana said, "it feels so freeing." Dana supposed that feeling weightless has had more of an emotional impact on her rather than a physical impact. "It feels great to interact with people at the same level," Dana articulated. In space, everyone is the same. Everyone moves in the same way and talks to each other eye-to-eye. In a way, Zero-G is a safe space that promotes equality. At that split 24-second mark, everything feels right with the world.

Systems Are Go

Mission AstroAccess is a relatively new organization with so much progress, so who knows what the future can hold? Dana Bolles predicts positive growth for Mission AstroAccess. "Based on where they started, when they selected Flight 1 ambassadors and today, I would say that they are just going to keep growing," Dana commented. Mission AstroAccess certainly has momentum, as there has been a macro push for people with disabilities to follow STEM careers worldwide. As for future aspirations, Dana speaks on behalf of the organization by saying they are looking to promote changes in equipment, policies, and procedures in the space industry. Dana is hopeful for a society with no social barriers for people with disabilities. Sooner or later, we may see space explorations pioneered or manned by astronauts with disabilities.

Houston, we have a problem.

Even with Mission AstroAccess pushing the envelope for disabled astronauts, Dana believes there is still much work to accomplish. Specifically, she thinks that the real challenge is what it takes for disabled astronauts to get chosen. "There is a lot that has to happen before we get to that point," said Dana, "it is not just floating around in space, which anybody could do." Dana highlighted, "in the selection, it is getting them not to be biased against you because you have a disability." Dana trusts that people with disabilities are just as capable as current astronauts. The real problem is convincing everyone else otherwise. "Being accepted and then getting selected," Dana concluded, "I would say the logistics of everything that leads up to that is the real challenge."

Another complication Dana considers about disabled astronaut crew is with training, such as zero gravity. People with disabilities need different types of exercise to accommodate their physical or mental needs. Dana explained one instance where she had trouble preparing for her Mission AstroAccess flight. "I needed to figure out how I was going to get from the floor of the plane to the seat," said Dana. "What happens on those flights is you start out sitting in the airplane seats," continued Dana, "right before you start doing the parabolas, you must go and lay down and wait. At the end of the set of parabolas, you must get back in your seat." Despite this challenge, Dana told me that it did not faze her. She attributes her bounce-back mentality to her independence and figuring out her life on the fly. Dana Bolles' final words were, "I am fine for now. Tomorrow we will see."

Chapter 12: Music and the Mission, Viktoria Modesta

Parmpreet Kang

Viktoria Modesta. This ambassador on the Mission AstroAccess project has left a mark on people not only through her music, but through her advocacy and passion to raise awareness and fight for the equality and inclusion of disabled people.

Who is Viktoria Modesta?

Viktoria Modesta is a 34 year old Latvian-born British singer and songwriter and has an extensive list of creative endeavours, including being a performance artist, creative director, social media influencer, and model.

Modesta was born with complications in her left leg due to her doctor's negligence during her birth (Wikipedia, n.d.). Her teenage mother faced pressure to send her to an orphanage but she saw her daughter for being more than her disability and chose to raise her. "My mum… saved me from being sent away somewhere" Modesta noted. Modesta continued to face stigma from a young age over her disability, with rude, unsolicited remarks from people, like "old ladies looking at you and saying, 'Oh my God, how are you gonna survive when you grow up, who is gonna marry you?'." However Modesta never let her disability and the harsh comments of others dissuade her from pursuing her passions and future pursuits.

In fact, at the young age of six, Viktoria had already began singing, and playing piano at a local music school in Daugavpils, Latvia (Wikipedia, n.d.). Then, at the age of 12, she moved with her family to the United Kingdom, where she has spent much of her adolescence and explored her interests. At 15 she became immersed in the world of modelling. She has been featured on multiple subculture magazines like Bizzare and SkinTwo as well as mainstream magazines like Vogue, Elle, and Harper's Bazaar (Wikipedia, n.d.). She has also done runway modelling for various fashion shows and as of 2015 has signed with IMG Models, a well-known international modelling agency.

Disability and Perseverance

In 2007, at the young age of 20, Viktoria made the brave and courageous decision to make a voluntary below-the-knee leg amputation in order to improve her mobility and protect her future health. "I genuinely felt I had a life as a new person. I upgraded my opportunities, my comfort, my body. It was really empowering" she said, in regards to getting the amputation. She then began to wear prosthetics, and continued to face criticism. "For a long time, pop culture closed its doors on me as an amputee and alternative artist. I think people have always found it hard to know what to think or feel about an amputee who wasn't trying to be an Olympian. In sports, 'overcoming' a disability makes you a hero, but in pop there is no place for these feelings" Viktoria stated (Channel 4, 2014). However, despite such hurdles, she continued to pursue her mission to make a name for herself in the music and entertainment industry and redefine the modern perception of beauty (Saner, n.d.). Viktoria began to use her prosthetic as a statement piece- a symbol of empowerment and artistic expression, branding herself as a "bionic pop artist". For instance, Viktoria was a part of the 2012 Summer Paralympics closing ceremony, where she performed "42" by Coldplay, wearing a prosthetic adorned in Swarovski crystals. In 2014, she collaborated with Channel 4, a British public service television network, for their 'Born Risky' brand campaign (Wikipedia, n.d.). She was branded as the first "Bionic Pop Artist" and released the song 'Prototype' for streaming on various platforms. The revolutionary and ahead-of-its-time music video for Prototype was posted on the Channel 4 website, and played during the X-Factor 2014 finale. The song and video aimed to showcase her disability in a unique and positive light, where Viktoria flaunts her disability and prosthetic limb and turns it into a powerful weapon. "Through this project with Channel 4's ' Born Risky', I'm hoping to set new principles in music and fashion, to rip up the rule book and develop a more empowering example of what it means to be a musician, model and artist" Viktoria said (Channel 4, 2014). The beginning of the video starts with the phrase "forget what you know about disability" written out, and unravels to spread a groundbreaking message- be proud of who you are, embrace your differences and don't let them limit you. The music video has received widespread global attention with over 16 million views on Channel 4's Facebook page and over 14 million views on YouTube as of September 2022.

Mission AstroAccess

Viktoria joined the Mission: AstroAccess project as one of the 12 disability ambassadors for the project. She has participated in the zero-gravity flight conducted by the team at 32, 000 ft above Earth. During the flight, Viktoria and her team conducted research and experiments, with a goal to better understand how space vessels and suits can be made more accessible for all people. Prior to the flight, one of Viktoria's tasks was to create the designs for the flight suits. She designed them to black with several zippers and pockets, and ensured the suits were customized with the needs of each ambassador in mind. "A lot of customization was done to people's flight suits, specifically with openings, pockets, extra straps, and different ways of helping their body function in zero gravity," Modesta shared (Grush, 2021). Tailoring the suits to the needs of the ambassadors was vital in ensuring they had a good experience aboard the flight. For instance, for one of the ambassadors, adding in special straps into their suit that held their legs together made it easier for them to focus on manoeuvring through the space for one of the ambassadors (Grush, 2021).

References

Wikipedia (n.d.). *Viktoria Modesta*. Retrieved September 7, 2022, from https://en.wikipedia.org/wiki/Viktoria_Modesta

Saner (2014, December 20). *Viktoria modesta, the world's first amputee pop star : 'if you don't fit in, then don't fit in'*. The Guardian. Retrieved September 7, 2022, from https://www.theguardian.com/music/2014/dec/20/-sp-amputee-pop-star-viktoria-modesta

Channel 4. *Channel 4 Presents World's First Bionic Pop Artist* | Channel 4. (2014, December 12). Retrieved September 7, 2022, from https://www.channel4.com/press/news/channel-4-presents-worlds-first-bionic-pop-artist

Chapter 13: A Conversation with Caitlin O'Brien

Benjamin A. Turner

Background

Mission: AstroAccess is made up of a diverse group of individuals from all walks of life. Caitlin O'Brien is passionate about science, currently an undergraduate student with Ohio State University she is studying Astrophysics & Astronomy, and Physics (Mission: AstroAccess). She is also passionate about advocating for accessibility, which ultimately led her to her work with SciAccess. Anna Voelker was Caitlin's advisor at Ohio State, she spoke with Voelker in March 2020 at an event and posed the idea of a portable planetarium for kids. Previous experience working on a portable planetarium inspired the idea, and her advisor agreed it was something they could look into.

The COVID-19 pandemic followed shortly thereafter, putting the planetarium idea to bed. "Suddenly the idea of putting a bunch of children in a closed bubble was a bad idea", O'Brien said. But the new reality of life under COVID also presented opportunities. In 2018 Voelker won the Ohio State University President's Prize (Ohio State University), and used the funding to found the organization SciAccess, whose mission was to promote equity in access to the sciences (SciAccess); a key part of that mission is the annual

SciAccess conference. In 2020 Voelker enlisted O'Brien to help with the organizing of that year's conference which needed to be remade in an entirely virtual format. O'Brien found herself attending planning sessions and quickly became the person who would volunteer to do just about anything. Her contribution involved planning, sending emails, and making phone calls. O'Brien couldn't help but smile when describing those first months of her involvement with SciAccess, it was a time when she wasn't sure what she had to contribute to the organization so she adopted a strategy of just agreeing to take on the tasks nobody else wanted.

During the conference, which was keynoted by Korean astronaut Dr. Yi Soyeon, O'Brien ran tech support. One of her major projects during the run-up was to contact every school in the United States for the blind and deaf that she could find to invite them to attend the virtual event. The conference was a success, if a bit of a whirlwind for O'Brien, and after it was done Voelker simply told O'Brien to "Have a nice day". Not satisfied, O'Brien asked her mentor what was next, and she was told to begin planning the 2021 conference.

This period following the 2020 SciAccess conference is when things really took off for O'Brien. In addition to helping organize the 2021 conference, she helped to found the Zenith Mentorship Program. She explained that in astronomy terms, zenith is the highest point, directly above the observer. The Zenith Mentorship program was designed to engage blind and visually impaired high school students from all over the world with student mentors from Ohio State University to engage them with astronomy and space sciences. It's an online program that creates the opportunity for young people who may not otherwise have access to the world of astronomy to expand their horizons.

Zero G Project

Around this time in 2020, O'Brien began attending conferences with Voelker and another student as a speaker. It was during these activities that O'Brien first encountered George Whitesides, former Chief Space Officer and Chief Executive Officer of Virgin Galactic. Whitesides soon began working with SciAccess on what was initially known as the Zero G Project, but eventually rebranded as Mission: AstroAccess. The general idea was to break down barriers to people with disabilities in space exploration by highlighting their unique abilities; highly qualified candidates with experience in space-related fields who also had physical disabilities would be engaged as program ambassadors. For the first flight, AstroAccess worked with 12 ambassadors who would get to experience zero-G through a service provided by a private contractor in California. Zero-G is achieved by flying repeated parabolic arcs, on the ascent passengers experience increased G-forces, but on the way down the illusion of zero-G is created because the aircraft is effectively in a state of freefall. The weightless sensation lasts for about 30 seconds at a time, and a typical flight repeats roughly forty arcs in a row.

The group planned several experiments for the flight, including demonstrations where ambassadors with prosthetic limbs removed and reattached the limbs in zero gravity. In another experiment, a visually impaired ambassador was wired up with a microphone and narrated where they believed themself to be in the aircraft as they drifted around, at the same time their position was recorded on video and compared to the recording of where the ambassador believed they were.

The purpose of the flight was to raise awareness and gain attention for the organization, thus boosting the advocacy efforts of SciAccess in their mission to highlight the antiquated nature of many space organizations thinking around disability. In fact, they argue, there are scenarios where a condition that would be considered a disability on Earth actually give a person an advantage in space. In other scenarios there are advantages to engaging with disabled people to increase the versatility of space operations. These ideas will be discussed further at the end of this chapter.

The first flight was a major milestone for Mission: AstroAccess, but also for O'Brien who described an overwhelming series of experiences. First, when invited to attend the launch she had no idea how she would get there; Voelker helped her draft an email to the staff of the Astronomy department at her school requesting funds to help with flights and accommodation. "I felt awkward about it because what I was doing wasn't even astronomy related, but I was asking astronomers for help", she said. But shortly after her email went out, a reply came back directing her to an office at the university that would help her with the funding, which she later received. "Once I got to California I was expecting lots of down time in my hotel room because I still didn't have a defined role; I actually brought my homework with me" O'Brien recalled. But once at the location she had no time for homework, there was work to do. As part of the ground crew she found herself managing accommodations, catering, and even media. The flight received media attention nationally and internationally, with outlets including the New York Times, National Public Radio, and the British Broadcast Corporation covering the story.

Most touching for O'Brien seems to be the sense of being a trusted team member. She fondly recounted how Whitesides was partly supporting the event financially, and when she had made the arrangements for the catering she was given his personal credit card to pay for the meals. "As an undergraduate student you're never given full control of anything, but there I was being given complete leeway over important parts of the event" O'Brien said. It's true that as young adults, many people are still basically treated like children. Those first experiences with trust and responsibility can be very impactful, and in the case of Ms. O'Brien, Mission: AstroAccess gave her those first important experiences. After the flight was completed, the sensation was a little surreal. O'Brien returned to her school, on her first day back she attended a quantum physics lecture and the world was carrying on as normal.

The return to normal life didn't last long, there were two subsequent flights that were the result of a partnership with the Aurelia Institute from the Massachusetts Institute of Technology (MIT). Aurelia invited one of the Mission: AstroAccess ambassadors to participate in a flight near Boston shortly after the first flight, and not long after that four ambassadors were given spots on a second flight. O'Brien and Voelker were on site as support crew for the second flight.

Collaboration, Not Charity

SciAccess and the project Mission: AstroAccess are not a charity group. O'Brien stressed the point that the organization is a collaborative one, they are not a group of non-disabled people gifting the experience to disabled people. It is very important to make the distinction, because ambassadors for Mission: AstroAccess are selected based on merit, their work and accomplishments are what qualify them to their positions. It is an organization of disabled and non-disabled people working side by side to engineer the experience for the ambassadors and to perpetuate their collective goals of advocating for people with auditory, visual, and mobility disabilities and their access to contribute to space exploration.

There exist many arbitrary and antiquated requirements to qualify for astronaut programs, and these barriers do more than stand in the way of disabled individuals. Space programs are weaker as a direct result of locking otherwise qualified candidates out of the process. Expanding space exploration with the planned Artemis missions to place a permanent station in Lunar orbit, and additionally to send humans to Mars will push space agencies and their staff to the most extreme limits any people have faced. O'Brien and SciAccess argue that arbitrarily limiting our capabilities by excluding some of our brightest minds makes the task more difficult and more expensive for everyone.

In one concrete example, O'Brien points to an incident in which Canadian astronaut Chris Hadfield was temporarily blinded during his first spacewalk on the International Space Station (Welsh). A suit malfunction led to soap getting into his eyes, the result was he lost his vision while working on the outside of the space station. This type of malfunction, if it had happened at the wrong time, could easily have been a fatal incident. Hadfield was able to work with the other astronaut on the spacewalk to resolve the issue, but what is frightening about the scenario is that while Hadfield was not incapacitated, he had full use of his limbs and mental faculties, there were no tools at his disposal that did not require hand-eye coordination. O'Brien notes that if NASA had worked with any visually impaired individuals, either as astronauts or as support crew, there would have been protocols in place that would have allowed Hadfield to handle the issue without necessarily triggering an emergency. This is precisely why SciAccess feels it is so important that accessibility be a consideration for space programs. The lived experience of an individual impacts the scenarios and solutions they can imagine, and sighted engineers at NASA may not have been the most effective people to consider a visual-impairment scenario for Colonel Hadfield. "One of the things Mission: AstroAccess ambassadors do is sit down and think, 'Why can't I be an astronaut?'" O'Brien said.

Thinking differently About Disability

There are many considerations that impact whether a disabled person should be allowed to apply to be an astronaut. We are entering a new era of space exploration with the Artemis program looking to return humans to the surface of the Moon in this decade, but also to act as the final weigh station for planned Mars missions in the 2030's (NASA). One of the points O'Brien makes is that if we are staffing a space station in orbit of the Moon on a permanent basis, we are certainly going to see issues around how to handle injuries in space; people with physical disabilities are uniquely qualified to troubleshoot such scenarios.

One example O'Brien points to is if an astronaut were to break a leg in Lunar orbit. The trip to Earth takes four days, but it is exceedingly unlikely there will be the capability to transport a person back to Earth for such an injury, they may even be required to serve the remaining months of their deployment before evacuation is possible, which would mean months of living with the injury in zero gravity. It is worth noting here that it would be an entirely new field of medical science to observe how bone heals in zero gravity. There is also no real understanding of how to put a cast on a limb in space. Setting a broken bone in space would also be an entirely new field of study. And once the injury is healed it is also unknown if the healing would be good enough without medical intervention once the astronaut returned to the Earth's gravity, it is conceivable that the injured limb would require surgery to re-break the bone and allow it to heal a second time to accommodate the additional stress of a gravity environment. "These are questions we do not have the answers to at the moment, but they are problems we will absolutely be facing as part of the Artemis mission." O'Brien stated.

O'Brien points out that one major area for concern with the current space program is muscular degeneration, particularly in the legs. "You see these videos of astronauts coming back to Earth and they can't even stand up because their muscles have degraded so badly." O'Brien noted. There is tremendous time and resources poured into keeping astronauts' legs healthy while they're in space because it is an important consideration for their overall health. One way to bypass this problem and extend their mission duration considerably could be to select an astronaut who is a paraplegic, or who doesn't have legs at all. The concern over atrophy would be completely moot if they don't have the use of their legs to begin with, and legs are almost completely useless in a zero-G environment. Under current program guidelines, persons with such disabilities would be automatically disqualified from consideration. If the individual is otherwise qualified, and this book is filled with examples of highly qualified individuals, then legs may not be a mission critical consideration.

One counterpoint to the proposal that legs are not necessary in space is cited by Ms. O'Brien: NASA is concerned that without the use of their legs, an astronaut would have difficulty affecting a bail-out scenario if their vessel encountered problems while in the atmosphere. It is a reasonable concern to raise, however it is also difficult to think that any serious thought has been put into the calculus of whether that risk outweighs the potential benefits of altering the entrance requirements for the astronaut program.

When considering the problem of muscular atrophy for astronauts staffing the space station, the mission duration is required to be relatively short. Somewhere between six months to one year. If that concern could be eliminated, then other, longer-term health impacts of zero gravity would be the primary factors setting the outer limits of mission duration. So if a Lunar space station could be staffed by an individual with a disability affecting leg mobility, their mission could be expanded potentially to several years in duration. Such a move could save billions of dollars of expense added by the requirement to ferry astronauts to and from the station several times over that period under the traditional rules. In this case there is a clear advantage for an astronaut who is not limited by the problem of muscular atrophy; indeed what is a disability on Earth could be a great asset in space.

What's Next

When discussing what's next for her, Ms. O'Brien says one important initiative she is currently working on is to advocate for the first deaf astronaut to be sent up on the Artemis mission. It would be an important victory for SciAccess and Mission: AstroAccess to be able to get that type of recognition for the deaf community.

As far as longer-term plans go, she points to the planned retirement of the International Space Station, and how there are three or four planned commercial initiatives for space stations currently in the works. She has been asked to work as low earth orbit destination liaison, "Which is a fancy way of saying I would talk to the space station" she quipped. She has made contact with the major players in the commercial space station sector and is hoping to continue her advocacy work on that front when those initiatives become the dominant force in low Earth orbit.

References

Mission: AstroAccess. "Organizing Team." *AstroAccess*, 20 July 2022, https://astroaccess.org/organizing-team/.

NASA. "Artemis." *NASA*, NASA, n.d., https://www.nasa.gov/specials/artemis/.

Ohio State University. "Ohio State Selects Two Scholars for 2018

President's Prize." *Ohio State Selects Two Scholars for 2018 President's Prize*, The Ohio State University, 12 July 2018, https://news.osu.edu/ohio-state-selects-two-scholars-for-2018-presidents-prize/.

SciAccess. "About SciAccess." *SciAccess,* 20 Mar. 2022, https://sciaccess.org/about-sciaccess/.

Welsh, Jennifer. "Astronaut Chris Hadfield Describes Being Blinded during a Space Walk." Business Insider, *Business Insider*, https://www.businessinsider.com/astronaut-chris-hadfield-ted-talk-blind-spacewalk-2014-3.

Chapter 14: Testing accessibility accommodations to for disabled or mixed-ability crews operating in space-like environments.

Dr. Jamie Molaro

Special note: the following chapter has been published by the Lunar Planetary Institute as a Conference Proceeding.

Introduction

Historically, disabled individuals have been excluded from human spaceflight opportunities in both the public and rapidly growing private sector due to perceptions that they lack the physical endurance or capacity to function in extreme environments, ability to perform rigorous or dexterous athletic activity, or the ability to operate effectively as part of a team with nondisabled individuals. Such perceptions born from pervasive and harmful societal assumptions about their ability to act and live independently and from the lack of motivation by individuals and institutions to make the necessary modifications to our physical environments and daily behaviors required make society more accessible. These assumptions are self-perpetuated by the fact that lack of accessible pathways to science and engineering careers leads to a decreased representation of disabled individuals who succeed in these communities.

We posit that with reasonable accommodations, as well as proper training for both disabled and nondisabled crew members, disabled individuals would not only be capable of performing the duties of an astronaut but would bring unique strengths to the role. Little research has been done to investigate how different disabilities may influence function in space-like environments or effective design principals for space vehicles and physical environments. On October 17, 2021 Mission: AstroAccess (MAA) [1] launched a group of disabled scientists, athletes, artists, and veterans on a ZERO-G Corporation parabolic flight to simulate weightlessness. These disabled "Ambassadors" carried out investigations to test accessibility accommodations that may assist future disabled astronauts operate in the extreme environment of space. Here we describe the demonstrations performed during the flight and learning outcomes.

Broad Goals

MAA has three broad goals to: (1) demonstrate that disabled individuals can successfully operate in a weightlessness, (2) test strategy and technology-based accommodations to enhance functionality in weightlessness, and (3) influence the policies of public and private space entities surrounding requirements for astronaut candidacy.

MAA Team

The mission is an initiative of SciAccess [2], an organization dedicated to advancing disability inclusion in STEM fields and led by co-author Voelker. The volunteer team is comprised of ~50 individuals at a wide range of career levels in academic, public, and private space-related sectors. The team was organized into several committees, though we will focus on activities within Flight Operations, which was led by author Molaro. Molaro joined MAA as a representative and the Director of Disabled for Accessibility In Space (DAIS) [3, 4], a peer networking group for disabled space professionals. Other partner organizations included Yuri's Night, Disabled American Veterans (DAV), the MIT Media Lab, and the American Institute of Aeronautics and Astronautics (AIAA).

Ambassadors and Disabilities

In addition to the ground team, twelve Ambassadors (Fig. 2) with a variety of backgrounds were selected to fly. For this flight, we specifically recruited individuals with disabilities in three categories: blind/low vision, deaf/hard of hearing, and mobility disabilities. Four Ambassadors had low vision with some light perception, and one was fully blind. Two Ambassadors were deaf. The remaining six Ambassadors had various types of mobility disabilities. Four of them were wheelchair users with limited to no control over lower limbs, and three of them used leg or arm prosthetics.

The demonstrations planned for each Ambassador on the flight were drafted by the ground team, relying on both disabled team members (including mission leadership) and team members with relevant expertise in disability issues prior to the Ambassador selections. Once selected, plans were finalized with input from the individual Ambassadors on their individual input.

Flight Plan and Description

The Zero-G aircraft flies in a parabolic trajectory that allows passengers to experience weightlessness. The experience has been likened to the weightless sensation that can occur while riding a roller coaster but is executed in a more controlled and precise manner. Our flight consisted of a set of 15 parabolas, each of which produced ~20-30 seconds of weightlessness. The duration of weightless periods is one of the primary challenges in executing zero-gravity investigations, as it requires any tasks to be executed very quickly. The first three parabolas consisted of two lunar and one martian gravity parabola to acclimate passengers to the physical sensation and prevent motion sickness.

The inside of the aircraft features a few rows of normal airplane seats, with the rest of the cabin open with a padded floor. Yoga mats were attached to the floor in the open area to designate "home" locations for each Ambassador. Straps and cords were attached to the walls, floor, and ceiling to use as hand and footholds. Other equipment for demonstrations was staged as needed after the flight took off.

Operational Challenges and Demonstrations

To plan the demonstrations performed on the flight, we explored the following question: What challenges does a weightless environment present to individuals and mixed-ability crews, and what technologies and operational strategies can we use to accommodate them? We focused our efforts on three primary areas of research: navigation, communication, and orientation.

Navigation. How do Ambassadors with any disability safely leave and return to their yoga mats? How do Ambassadors with partial or full paralysis maintain limb control against inertial forces? How do Ambassadors with mobility disabilities station-keep in microgravity? Demonstrations included cables and handholds to assist in translation and use of rigid canes for reach and stabilization. Flight suit modifications were also tailored specifically individuals to assist in limb control (e.g., a strap to secure legs together) and facilitate access to or stowage of prosthetics (e.g., straps to secure a prosthetic to the body).

Communication. How do deaf Ambassadors receive critical communication from flight crew about changing conditions? Is ASL possible with different (e.g., upside down) or changing (e.g., tumbling) orientations? Does signing impart momentum? Demonstrations included light beacons and haptic (vibration) devices to signal change in gravity status, as well as testing viability of ASL during off-nominal orientation. *Orientation.* How do blind Ambassadors collect information to provide location awareness within the cabin? How do blind Ambassadors orient themselves for movement when their position is unknown? Demonstrations included sound beacons for locating the front of the aircraft, haptic devices (as for deaf Ambassadors), tactile markers to indicate directionality on wall surfaces, and haptic devices providing proximity warnings for obstacles.

Demonstration Outcomes

We found that most Ambassadors needed little physical intervention during the flight, commensurate with non-disabled passengers per the Zero-G flight attendants, and that all Ambassadors were regularly able to return independently to their yoga mats when coming out of weightlessness. The handholds and cables were useful for all Ambassadors, though canes were found to impart too much momentum. The flight suit modifications were very successful.

Deaf Ambassadors reported that ASL communication was possible in various orientations, but difficult to test due to the fact that their hands were frequently in use for station-keeping. The light beacons had limited success for communicating change in gravity because there were not enough in the cabin to ensure one could see them from any orientation. However, Ambassadors reported that the haptic feedback signal was clear regardless of orientation and feel the technology is highly promising. In both cases, one issue with our implementation was that relay of information from the pilot to the device operator resulted in a signal delay, however this can be easily overcome by better automating the process.

The sound beacons did not work for Blind Ambassadors because the airplane cabin was too boisy to hear them. Future tests could be done by routing sound to crew through noise-cancelling earbuds. Ambassadors attempted to use other people in the cabin as sound markers, however this proved difficult because they could not tell if the person they were hearing was stationary or in motion. Haptic feedback for navigation had little success largely due to the large number of obstacles (people, walls, etc) around them (i.e., if a proximity sensor is always going off the information is not useful). Such technology may have promise but needs more innovation and ground testing.

Future Research: We will report our findings and discuss future research directions, including additional flights, further development and ground-testing of promising technologies, and research campaigns aimed at understanding the challenges faced by people with types of disabilities not represented on flight one.

References

[1] Voelker, A. et al., www.astroaccess.org. [2] Voelker, A., et al., www.sciaccess.org. [3] Molaro, J.L. (2021) AGU Fall Meeting, #SH34A-03. [4] Molaro, J.L., www.disabledinspace.org.

Figure 1. Ambassadors in front of the Zero-G plane before boarding. From left to right is (top row) Mary Cooper, Sheri Wells-Jensen, Eric Shear, Apurva Varia, Sina Bahram, Zuby Onwuta, Mona Minkara, Viktoria Modesta, (bottom row) Sawyer Rosenstein, Dana Bolles, Eric Ingram, and Ce-Ce Mazyck. (from internal communications)

Conclusion

Peter Anto Johnson

The concept of disabled people traveling to space has been one explored in much of science fiction for decades but an idea that has received much pushback. Challenges such as dealing with dynamic accelerations, changes in g force, and weightlessness are all significant to consider. Additionally, in space, the human physiology is highly vulnerable to demands such as exposure to inert gases and extremely low atmospheric pressure even for those without disabilities. Current treatment capabilities in space are also limited with the survivability and management of acute conditions being much more difficult than on ground. Nevertheless, ability is relative. There are a continuum of disabilities that affect different individuals variably. Moreover, individuals who have dreamed of space, invested their energy into training, knowledge, and skills acquisition are denied an opportunity due to a label from society. Mission AstroAccess is a step forward. For health. For progress. For the world. For humanity.

www.ingramcontent.com/pod-product-compliance
Lightning Source LLC
Chambersburg PA
CBHW030118170426
43198CB00009B/665